Angels of Mercy

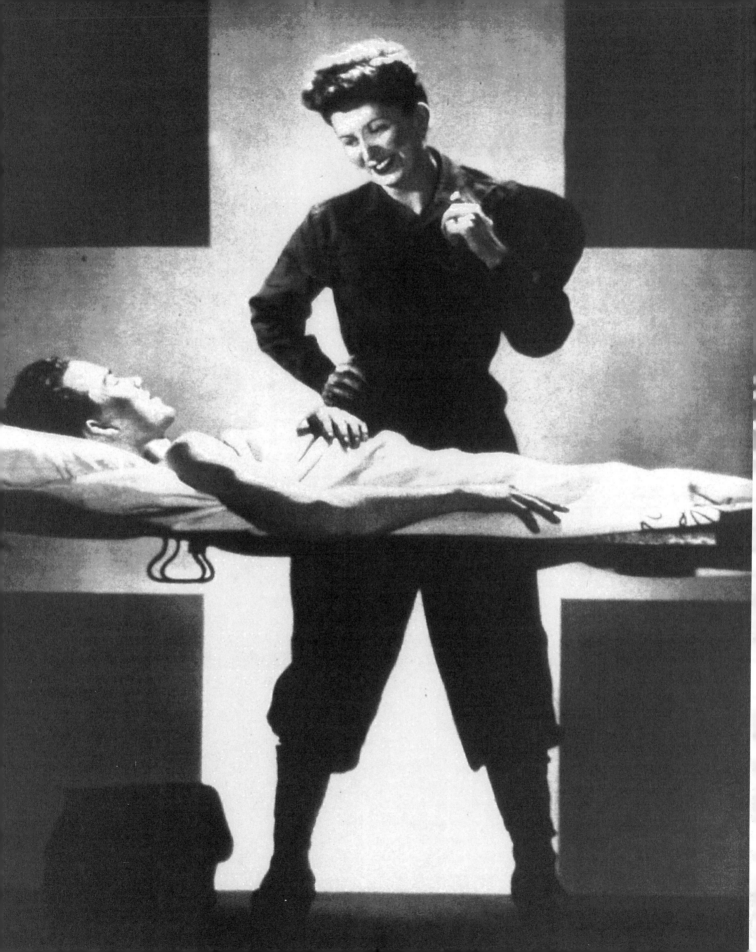

Angels of Mercy

by

BETSY KUHN

 The ARMY NURSES of WORLD WAR II

ATHENEUM BOOKS for YOUNG READERS

AUTHOR'S NOTE TO WORLD WAR II ARMY NURSES

It has been a privilege to tell the story of World War II Army nurses, and I only hope I have done the job justice. Note that I have left out references to rank for the most part because I don't think young readers care much about that sort of thing. Also, I've focused on nurses who served near the front lines not because their work was more important than that of nurses farther back, but because their units' movements so closely reflected the progress of the war. Finally, I've had to leave out many stories. If I've missed something important, or described an event differently than you remember, I apologize. Please know that I did the best I could drawing from interviews and research. I've loved telling your story, and I admire every one of you.   —B. K.

Atheneum Books for Young Readers   An imprint of Simon & Schuster Children's Publishing Division 1230 Avenue of the Americas   New York, New York 10020   Text copyright © 1999 by Betsy Kuhn All rights reserved, including the right of reproduction in whole or in part in any form.   Book design by Michael Nelson   The text of this book is set in Centennial.   Printed in the United States of America 2   4   6   8   10   9   7   5   3   1
Library of Congress Cataloging-in-Publication Data   Kuhn, Betsy.   Angels of Mercy: the Army nurses of World War II / by Betsy Kuhn.—1st ed.   p. cm.   Includes bibliographical references and index. Summary: Relates the experiences of World War II Army nurses, who brought medical skills, courage, and cheer to hospitals throughout Europe, North Africa, and the Pacific.   ISBN 0-689-82044-5 1. World War, 1939-1945—Medical care—United States—Juvenile literature.   2. United States. Army Nurse Corps—Biography—Juvenile literature.   3. World War, 1939-1945—Personal narratives, American—Juvenile literature.   4. Nurses—United States—Biography—Juvenile literature.   [1. World War, 1939-1945—Medical care. 2. United States. Army Nurse Corps—Biography. 3. World War, 1939-1945—Personal narratives, American. 4. Nurses.]   I. Title.   D807.U6K84 1999 940.54'7673'0922—dc21   98-36610

Frontispiece: *National Archives*

FIRST EDITION

IN LOVING MEMORY OF MY AUNT,

June Bossler;

TO

Alice,
with love and admiration;

AND TO

Phoebe, of course,
with love and thanks.
—B.K.

ACKNOWLEDGMENTS

The author would like to thank the following people for their help with this book: Phoebe Miller, Edwinna Bernat, Major Constance J. Moore (former Army Nurse Corps historian and an unfailing source of help and enthusiasm); Brigadier General Wilma Vaught, Kathryn Sheldon, Judith Bellafaire, Britta Granrud, and Marlene Murty of the Women's Memorial (WIMSA); Rich Boylan, National Archives; Sidney Butterfield, Julian Egnaczewski, Austin Fernald, James A. Taylor; Nancy Wheeler and Terri Collins, *Poolesville Community News;* Mark Gochnour, Poolesville Library, Poolesville, Maryland; Mary Thomas, Lieutenant Colonel Debulon Bell, U.S. Army Center of Military History; and Edward Harkness.

A special thank you goes to the following World War II Army nurses: June Bossler, Alice Weinstein, Erna Thompson, Hattie R. Brantley, Prudence Burns Burrell, Anna Williams Clark, Claudine Glidewell Doyle, Ruby Duff, Nola Forrest, Henrietta Harkness, Grace Hunn, Helen Dixon Johnson, Orpha Warner Johnson, Marcella Schlemma Korda, Agnes Jensen Mangerich, June Wandrey Mann, Maureen J. Martin, Ramona Music McCormick, Helen M. Nestor, Sally Hocutt Offutt, Helen Molony Reichert, Vera J. Lee Rieck, Elma Rinehart, Hildegarde M. Wright, and Pauline Sommars Zupan.

And on the home front, thanks as always to Greg for his support and good humor; to Royan Miller; and to Michael and Nicholas for all their smiles and more.

✪ TABLE OF CONTENTS ✪

☆ TIME LINE ☆

EUROPE & NORTH AFRICA		PACIFIC
	1939 September 1	
Germans invade Poland: World War II begins		
	1940 June September	
Fall of France "The Blitz": Germans bomb London		
	1941 December 7 December 8	Japanese attack Pearl Harbor USA enters war
	1942 April 9 May 6	Fall of Bataan, Philippines Fall of Corregidor, Philippines; 66 Army nurses taken prisoner

Allies invade North Africa; nurses
    with the 48th Surgical Hospital land
    with the troops
	November 8	

	1943 July 9–10 September 3 September 9 September 13	
Allies invade Sicily Italy surrenders Allies invade Italy at Salerno USS *Newfoundland* bombed off Salerno with nurses aboard		

EUROPE & NORTH AFRICA		PACIFIC

1944

Allies land at Anzio, Italy	January 22	
Nurses arrive at Anzio	January 27–28	
95th Evac. Hospital at Anzio bombed	February 7	
Allies march into Rome	June 4	
D day: Allies invade Normandy, France	June 6	
Nurses begin arriving on Normandy beaches	June 10	
Allies invade southern France	August 15	
	October 20	Americans invade Philippines
	November 1	Nurses arrive on Philippines
Battle of the Bulge begins	December 16	

1945

	February	POW nurses liberated in the Philippines
Allied troops cross Germany's Rhine River	March 7	
Nurses of the 51st Field Hospital cross Rhine	March 13	

April 12
President Roosevelt dies; Harry Truman becomes President

	April 28	USS *Comfort* hospital ship bombed
Hitler commits suicide	April 30	
Germany surrenders	May 7	
	August 6	Atomic bomb dropped on Hiroshima
	August 9	Atomic bomb dropped on Nagasaki
	August 14	Japan surrenders
	September 2	Japan signs surrender; war ends

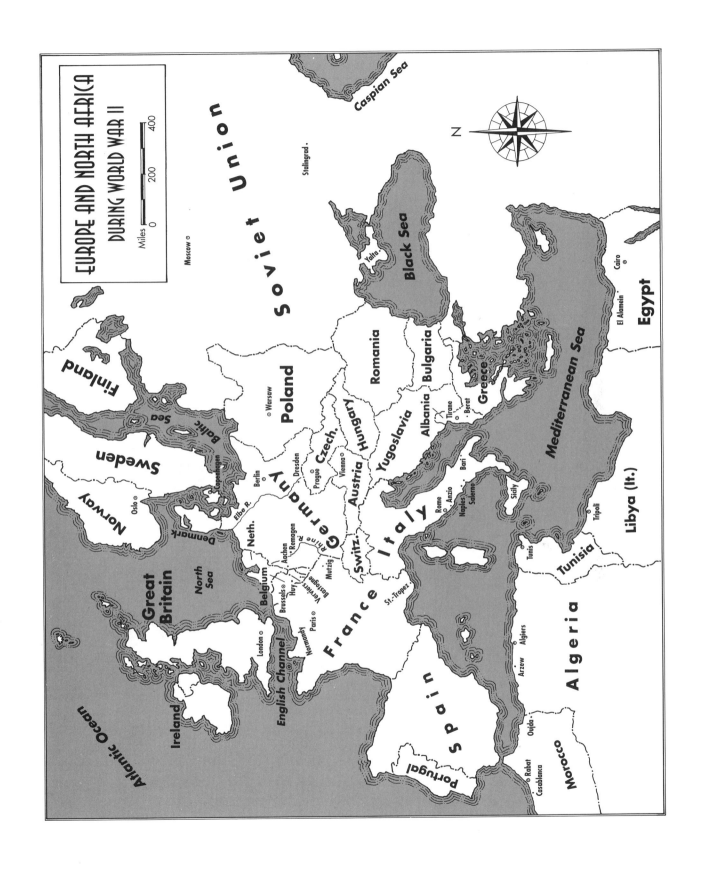

EUROPE AND NORTH AFRICA
DURING WORLD WAR II

Miles
0   200   400

Atlantic Ocean

Ireland

Great Britain

North Sea

London

English Channel

Normandy

Paris

France

Belgium

Brussels

Verviers

Huy

Bastogne

Metzig

Aachen

Remagen

Rhine

Neth.

Elbe R.

Denmark

Berlin

Germany

Dresden

Prague

Czech.

Vienna

Austria

Switz.

Copenhagen

Baltic Sea

Oslo

Sweden

Norway

Finland

Poland

Warsaw

Soviet Union

Moscow

Stalingrad

Caspian Sea

Black Sea

Yalta

Romania

Hungary

Yugoslavia

Albania

Bulgaria

Tirane

Berat

Greece

Italy

Rome

Anzio

Naples

Salerno

Bari

Sicily

Mediterranean Sea

St. Tropez

Spain

Portugal

Rabat

Casablanca

Morocco

Oujda

Arzew

Algiers

Algeria

Tunis

Tunisia

Tripoli

Libya (It.)

El Alamein

Cairo

Egypt

N

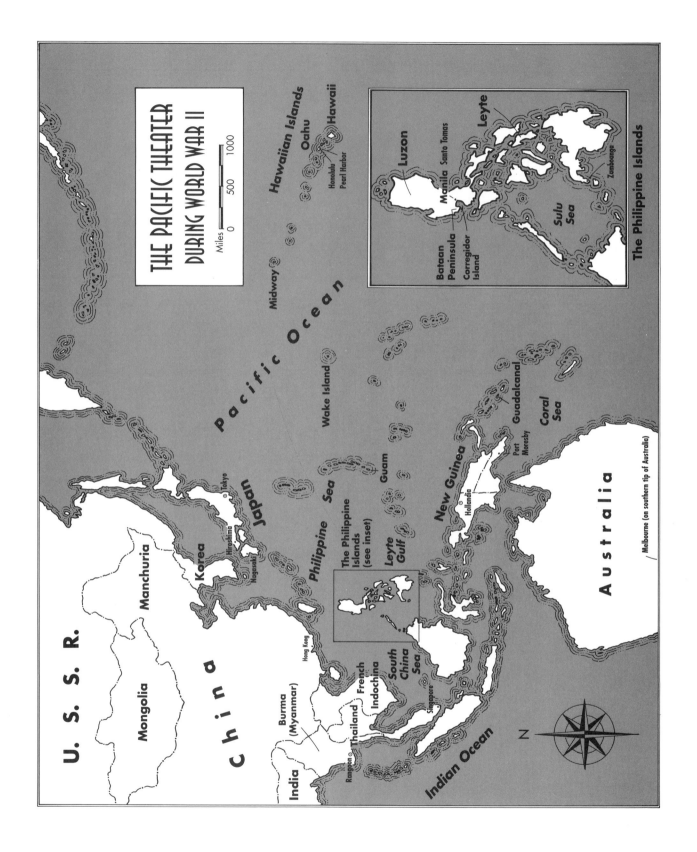

THE PACIFIC THEATER
DURING WORLD WAR II

Miles
0   500   1000

Hawaiian Islands
Oahu
Honolulu
Pearl Harbor
Hawaii

Midway

Pacific Ocean

Wake Island

Philippine Sea

Guam

The Philippine Islands (see inset)

Leyte Gulf

New Guinea
Hollandia

Port Moresby

Guadalcanal

Coral Sea

Australia

Melbourne (on southern tip of Australia)

N

Indian Ocean

Singapore

South China Sea

French Indochina

Thailand

Burma (Myanmar)

Rangoon

India

China

Hong Kong

Korea

Japan
Tokyo
Hiroshima
Nagasaki

Manchuria

Mongolia

U. S. S. R.

The Philippine Islands

Luzon

Manila
Santo Tomas
Bataan Peninsula
Corregidor Island

Leyte

Zamboanga

Sulu Sea

Angels of Mercy

one

⟫1941⟪

"WHAT IN THE WORLD
IS GOING ON?"

MILDRED IRENE CLARK: "IT'S MANEUVERS"

FOR MILDRED IRENE CLARK, DECEMBER 7, 1941, WAS SUPPOSED TO BE A day off. She was going to clean her room, and later planned to go horseback riding with friends. But Clark was an Army nurse stationed near Pearl Harbor, on the Hawaiian island of Oahu, and just before 8 A.M., her plans changed fast.

It was a warm and sunny Sunday morning. Clark was still in bed when suddenly hundreds of planes swarmed across the island. Without warning, they began to drop load after load of bombs. They soared over Pearl Harbor, home of the U.S. Pacific Fleet, attacking battleships and destroyers. They fired on the fighter planes, parked wing tip to wing tip at Wheeler Field, next to Schofield Barracks, where Mildred Clark lived.

The bombs sent her hurrying to the window. "I could see planes and they were getting closer," she says. "I could see all the smoke rising. It was black and the bombs were exploding over toward Wheeler Field. I called the Operating Room and said, 'What in the world is going on?'

1

"Another nurse answered, 'I don't know, but it sounds terrible.'"[1]

All over Oahu, other people were just as confused. It's maneuvers, some insisted, just the Army Air Force taking their planes out for a run. But how did that explain the bombs? The torpedoes barreling into the sides of the powerful battleships?

Clark didn't know what the bombs meant, but she knew she had work to do. She was an anesthetist, one of only three at Schofield Station Hospital. Quickly, she dressed in her operating-room outfit—she didn't even stop to brush her teeth—and ran out of the dormitory toward the operating room.

The Japanese attack on Pearl Harbor cost the Americans more than 2,400 lives and destroyed ships and aircraft. *(Corbis-Bettman)*

"The planes were right over me. I could see two men [in them]. I don't remember being afraid, but I thought, what in the world are those apples on the planes for?"

Those weren't apples! That big red circle was the Japanese symbol for the Rising Sun. The Japanese were attacking Pearl Harbor!

By the time Clark reached the hospital, the casualties were already lined up in the corridors on stretchers. They were laid out in the operating rooms, and more and more were arriving by ambulance. Many patients had lost arms and legs. Others had suffered terrible burns, or severe stomach or chest wounds. Chaplains administered last rites to dying men.

The first Japanese attack lasted about a half hour. A second attack followed. By 10 A.M., the air raid was all over. More than 2,400 Americans had been killed and 1,000 more wounded. The Japanese had destroyed battleships and airplanes. The battleship *Arizona,* hit twice, exploded in flame and then quickly sank; more than 1,000 men on board were killed, many of them trapped below deck.

The Japanese didn't stop there, though. They also struck British and American military bases in the Philippines, Midway, Wake Island, Guam, Hong Kong, and Singapore.

The attacks took nearly everyone by surprise even though tensions had been high between the United States and Japan. All through the fall, the two countries had been negotiating: The United States wanted Japan to pull its troops out of China and stop attacking other Far Eastern countries, but Japan's prime minister, General Hideki Tojo, was also minister of war. Not only would he not withdraw troops, he wanted to claim even more land for Japan. With the attack on Pearl Harbor, the Japanese hoped to make the United States too weak to interfere.

Few Americans expected war. It didn't seem possible that tiny Japan would attack the powerful United States, and U.S. citizens had made it very clear to President Franklin D. Roosevelt that they did not want another war after the horrors of World War I. In Europe, Adolf Hitler was taking over one country after another. Still, most Americans considered that a European problem.

At the Schofield Station Hospital on Oahu, Mildred Clark worked all day without a break. The operating room was hot, like a sweatbox, and supplies ran short.

"We will gain the inevitable triumph, so help us God," said President Franklin D. Roosevelt, shown here signing the declaration of war against Japan. (Franklin D. Roosevelt Library)

At six o'clock someone set out fried chicken and rolls. Clark hadn't eaten all day, but she wasn't hungry. She'd seen so much, done so much, she couldn't possibly eat. She had a cup of black coffee, nothing more.

The next day, President Roosevelt spoke before Congress as citizens listened on radios all across the country.

"Yesterday, December 7, 1941—a day which will live in infamy—the United States was suddenly and deliberately attacked," he said. The United States declared war on Japan, and within days, Germany and Italy declared war on the United States. Now the United States, Great Britain, and the Soviet Union (Russia) were allies in the fight against the Axis powers of Germany, Italy, and Japan.

Mildred Clark was still too busy treating casualties to hear FDR's stirring speech. For two weeks, she couldn't even call her parents in the States to assure them that she was okay because military communications took priority. She was so busy at the hospital that she stayed there continuously for three weeks, which was fine by her. The Geneva Cross on the roof made it the safest place on base.

The Geneva Cross, or the Red Cross, identifies a hospital as a neutral facility under the terms of a group of treaties known as the Geneva Conventions. Medical staff and patients are neutral parties, not fighters, and are not to be hurt. Countries that have signed the treaties agree to abide by their terms. The International Red Cross was founded in Europe as a direct result of the first Geneva treaty. Clara Barton, founder of the American Red Cross, persuaded the United States to sign the treaty in 1882.

In Hawaii, the rumors were flying like crazy. The Japanese were about to land troops on Oahu! They were going to attack San Francisco! The military imposed martial law on Hawaii calling for curfews and blackouts. At night, the hospital staff hung blankets over the windows to block the light, so the enemy couldn't spot targets. Everyone on the island was issued a gas mask and fined five dollars if they were caught without it.

It was a difficult time, but in some ways, Mildred was lucky. Once the Japanese left Hawaii, they didn't come back. That wasn't the case in the Philippines, where the nurses had a very different story to tell.

AN ORDEAL IN THE PHILIPPINES:
THE JAPANESE ATTACK

In 1941, the nearly one hundred Army nurses stationed in the Philippine Islands considered themselves lucky. This Pacific paradise, thousands of miles from home, was a choice assignment where the nurses enjoyed warm weather, palm trees, fragrant hibiscuses, and all the mangoes they could eat. The United States had acquired the Philippines in 1898 at the close of the Spanish-American War, and the country was now home to a number of U.S. Army and Navy bases, as well as several Army hospitals.

Most nurses served at Sternberg General Hospital in the beautiful old city of Manila on the island of Luzon, while a small number served on the island of Corregidor. Corregidor, known as "the Rock," was covered with dense jungle, but underneath the wild foliage lay a vast underground complex known as the Malinta Tunnel. Here were headquarters for the command of the U.S. Pacific forces, ammunition storage, and a hospital.

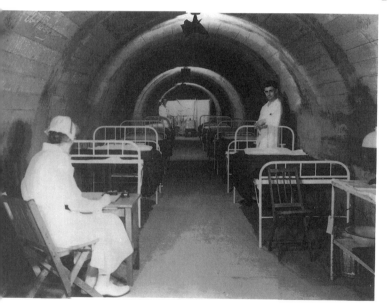

The Malinta Tunnel Hospital on Corregidor before the war. These beds would never be this empty once the Japanese attacked the Philippines. *(Army Nurse Corps, U.S. Army Center of Military History)*

Throughout 1941, as rumors of tension between the United States and Japan increased, the Army conducted air raid drills and issued helmets and gas masks. Few of the servicepeople worried much; the islands of the Philippines were well fortified by the military. General Douglas MacArthur had thousands of U.S. and Filipino troops under his command. Most people believed the Japanese would never dare attack them.

But the Japanese began bombing Luzon on December 8, the same day they struck Hawaii (the Philippine Islands lie on the other side of the international date line). They bombed U.S. planes at Clark Field, north of Manila, destroying the island's air power.

"They bombed Cavite, the Navy base there," remembers nurse Rose Meier. "And they started bringing in wounded, oh, just by the truckloads." Patients had to be laid out on the lawn. "They were just mangled and shot to pieces."[2]

But the Japanese didn't stop bombing the Philippines after one day as they had Pearl Harbor, Hawaii. They launched air raid after air raid. Soon thousands of Japanese troops had landed on the north coast of Luzon and were marching south toward Manila. With its airplanes destroyed, MacArthur's army could not stop them.

By mid-December, the Japanese had gained so much ground that the nurses at outer bases were ordered to Manila.

Two nurses stationed at tiny Camp John Hay in northern Luzon headed south for Manila on foot, hiking for thirty hours over difficult mountain trails. Then the Japanese caught up with them when they stopped to treat civilians at a sawmill camp, and they became POWs: prisoners of war.

In the meantime, MacArthur was sending his troops to the Bataan Peninsula, in western Luzon, to wage an all-out stand against the Japanese. He expected more U.S. troops would soon arrive to reinforce his men, and they would easily drive the enemy from the Philippines.

On Christmas Eve, twenty-five nurses left Manila by bus to set up a hospital on Bataan. They weren't allowed to bring much. They packed extra uniforms, a few photographs, and their white duty shoes. They passed villages ruined by war, abandoned rice paddies, and weary Filipino families fleeing the Japanese.

The Japanese "were going over us, striking us and bombing us all the time," says Rose Meier. "We had to run and get out of the bus and get on the hillside." And yet the nurses were so glad to be out of Manila and the crowded hospital that many felt almost lighthearted.

When the group stopped to buy bananas, one soldier bought some food cooked by a villager even though the Army strongly recommended that nobody buy food cooked outside Army kitchens.

One of the nurses warned he might get sick, that the food might have worms!

"Listen, sister," he fired back. "You'll be eating worse than this before the party's over and be glad to get it."[3]

The nurses simply laughed.

CHRISTMAS/HANUKKAH, 1941

The nurses who arrived on Bataan on Christmas Eve had their work cut out for them. "We were told we were going to a well-established hospital," says Edith Corn Lloyds. "Were they ever wrong on that one. What we found . . . was a vacated Philippine Army Quartermaster Depot." All around them were mountains and thick stands of banyan and eucalyptus trees, bamboo, and vines.

The nurses spent Christmas Day cleaning their new hospital and setting up beds for patients. Just a month before, they'd felt lucky to live in this island paradise. Now the Japanese were closing in on Bataan.

THE ARMY NURSE CORPS IN WORLD WAR II

More than fifty-nine thousand Army nurses served in World War II. In fact, in all, approximately four hundred thousand American women served in the war, more than in any other conflict before or since, but the nurses saw more action and served in more places than any other servicewomen. Army nurses came from all over the United States—from the tiniest towns to the biggest cities—often to serve in places they'd never heard of: Oujda, Aachen, Zamboanga. They served throughout Europe, North Africa, and the Pacific. They served in the ice fields of Alaska and the jungles of New Guinea. They served on land, and on hospital ships and trains. For the first time ever in a war, they served on airplanes, helping to evacuate the wounded.

Almost all of them joined the Army Nurse Corps because they wanted to serve their country. Some hoped for adventure as well, but they soon learned the war was real. A nurse could be wounded, taken prisoner, even killed. More than two hundred Army nurses died during World War II. Some were taken prisoner and held for years.

Like the nurses at Pearl Harbor and the Philippines, though, they knew they had a job to do. They had to keep "our boys" fit to fight; they had lives to save. The nurses brought more than medical skills to their posts; they brought courage and cheer to the darkest places, in the grimmest periods of the war, and in so doing, they earned a nickname: Angels of Mercy.[4]

two

⟫1942⟪

REPORTING FOR DUTY

BY EARLY 1942, THE UNITED STATES WAS IN THE THICK OF WORLD WAR II. But understanding how this happened begins with Europe, and the end of World War I. The Germans had started that war, and they'd lost. According to the Versailles Treaty of 1919, the German military was to be severely limited. The Germans had to admit the war was their fault, and they had to make large cash payments to the countries that had defeated them.

Because of this, and other problems, the German economy was a wreck; many Germans were out of work. The country was ripe for a new leader.

Adolf Hitler, head of the Nazi Party, declared that Germany was the greatest country on earth and Germans the greatest race. They were superior to other countries in Europe and shouldn't have to do what they were told by them. Many Germans liked what he had to say, and in 1933, Hitler became dictator of Germany.

Then he began to inflict the cost of his leadership. Those who disagreed with him often lost their jobs or were imprisoned or killed, so when Hitler started persecuting the Jews, few people

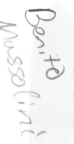

e against him. The Jews, he said, were to blame for Ger-
'____s troubles, and many agreed. He proclaimed they had no
____ ____nong Germans, the "master race."

____ ____an Jews lost all their rights. They were shunned, even
____ ____n, their businesses ruined. Unfortunately, that was just the
beginning. Ultimately, Hitler's plan was to eliminate the Jews
entirely.

Soon it was not enough for Hitler to lord his power over Germany. He built up the military, defying the Versailles Treaty. In
1938, the Nazis took over neighboring German-speaking Austria,
then Czechoslovakia.

Leaders in France and Great Britain became alarmed. For a
long time, they had failed to take Hitler seriously, but now he had
a powerful army at his command and his sights were set on
Poland.

Britain and France promised to help Poland if Germany
attacked. When one million German troops invaded Poland on
September 1, 1939, France and Great Britain declared war on
Germany: World War II had begun.

Poland fell to the Nazis in about a month. By the end of 1940,
the Nazis had taken control of Norway, Belgium, Denmark, even
France.

Then they turned their attention to Great Britain. In September 1940, they launched "the Blitz," bombing London and other
cities again and again, and expecting the British to surrender.

But the British didn't give up. Under their new prime minister,
Winston Churchill, they withstood everything the Germans gave
them. Eventually, the Germans backed off—but not for good.

There was another dictator in Europe, Benito Mussolini of
Italy. Like Hitler, he sought power beyond his own country and

invaded first Ethiopia in Africa, then Albania, a tiny country across the Adriatic Sea.

Adolf Hitler (foreground) and Benito Mussolini led the Axis powers in Europe. (Hulton-Deutsch Collection/ Corbis)

In 1936, Mussolini and Hitler joined forces. Germany and Italy became known as the Axis powers along with one other country: Japan.

On the other side of the globe, the Japanese were waging war on other countries, just as the Germans were. The Japanese military leaders who held most of the power were looking beyond the tiny islands that make up Japan for more land to handle the country's growing population. They wanted the rich resources, like rubber and oil, found in the nations of Southeast Asia.

In 1931, the Japanese invaded Manchuria, in northeastern China, and eventually seized control of major Chinese cities and ports. In 1940, they invaded Indochina, the peninsula between India and China, including Burma (now Myanmar).

Slowly but surely, the Land of the Rising Sun, as Japan is known, was gaining power in Asia and the Pacific. Under General Hideki Tojo, the prime minister of Japan, the country would gain more.

Americans, on the other hand, had had their fill of war with World War I, which was supposed to be "the War to End All Wars." While many Americans were concerned about the Europeans' plight, they had no desire to take up arms against Hitler. The United States was trying to recover from the Great Depression, and many citizens, known as isolationists, opposed helping foreign countries at all.

President Franklin D. Roosevelt warned that if the United States failed to help the Allies, the Axis powers would gain control of the oceans and limit shipping between the Allies and among other nations. At his urging, the United States became an "arsenal of democracy," supplying the Allies with badly needed tanks, planes, and other war supplies.

Still, as much as the war loomed in the news, it didn't really hit home until December 7, 1941.

"I regret to tell you that many American lives have been lost," President Roosevelt told the country after the Pearl Harbor attack. He didn't have to worry about isolationists anymore as now almost every citizen was ready to do his or her part to help win the war.

THE 95TH EVACUATION HOSPITAL:
"YOU ARE NEEDED NOW"

All over the United States, people were asking themselves what they could do for the war effort. For Sally Hocutt, a nurse from North Carolina, the answer was spelled out in the big recruiting posters. "You Are Needed Now," they said. "Join the Army Nurse Corps."

With the war under way, the Army was recruiting nurses through the American Red Cross. So in 1942, at age twenty-one, Hocutt applied through the Red Cross, then reported to the Army.

"What's your name?" asked the man from the Army.

YOU ARE NEEDED NOW

JOIN THE
ARMY NURSE CORPS
APPLY AT YOUR RED CROSS RECRUITING STATION

"S. Jewel Hocutt," she replied since Jewel was what they called her at home.

But he needed her first name, Sally.

"Please," she said, "I prefer to be S. Jewel Hocutt."

Sorry, he told her, you can't use a middle name.

"Well, the generals can," she pointed out.

"Honey," he said with a smile, "you aren't a general."

Clearly, Hocutt had a lot to learn about the Army, as did Pauline Sommars of Wadena, Minnesota, another new recruit in the Army Nurse Corps. She hoped to serve overseas. Then, she says, "Two of my friends were sent to Alaska. I thought, oh gosh, I don't want to go to Alaska. I want to go where the excitement is!"

She got her wish and then some. She and Sally Hocutt were both assigned to the 95th Evacuation Hospital and would serve in Africa and Europe in some of the war's most dangerous spots.

When the United States entered the war, Sally Hocutt knew where she was needed. *(Sally J. Offutt)*

Opposite page: After the Pearl Harbor attack, the Army Nurse Corps recruited more than ten thousand nurses in six months. *(National Archives)*

Clara Barton cared for Union soldiers on Civil War battlefields. *(ANC/U.S. Army)*

Serving in the military was a new experience for Sally and Pauline, but wartime nursing was nothing new. Women had served as nurses during the Revolutionary War, earning eight dollars a month. And in the Civil War, they'd cared for the Union and Confederate Armies, although few of them had any medical training.

Louisa May Alcott, author of *Little Women*, was a Civil War nurse, but perhaps the most famous nurse was Clara Barton. She fearlessly cared for Union soldiers in some of the war's fiercest battles, including Antietam and Bull Run.

During the Spanish-American War in 1898, Army nursing assumed a more formal role. More than fifteen hundred male and female nurses were organized by Dr. Anita Newcomb McGee, and for the first time, they were all fully trained. They served as far away as Cuba, Puerto Rico, and the Philippines, where they faced water shortages and diseases as they cared for the wounded and dying, just as many nurses would later in World War II.

The nurses proved to be so valuable that it was clear they deserved an official place in the Army. Thus, the Army Nurse Corps was established in 1901.

The Corps grew in importance during World War I. More than twenty-one thousand women served as Army nurses, and more

More than twenty-one thousand Army nurses served in World War I, including approximately ten thousand who served overseas. *(ANC/U.S. Army)*

than ten thousand of them went overseas to places like France, Belgium, and England.

With World War II, the Army Nurse Corps, under Superintendent Julia O. Flikke, faced its biggest challenge yet. At the time of the Pearl Harbor attack, there were fewer than one thousand nurses in the corps. But *thousands* were needed. So, with the help of the Red Cross, the corps worked hard to recruit new volunteers.

A nurse had to be a female between twenty-one and forty years of age. (Later, the age limit was raised to forty-five.) She entered the corps as an officer, usually a second lieutenant, but held only relative rank, meaning she earned less and enjoyed fewer privileges than her male counterparts in the Army. (In fact, it wasn't until 1947 that Army nurses were granted the same rank and privileges as male officers.)

Patients at Bataan's Hospital #2 slept out in the open. "If we needed more room," says Rose Meier, "we got our axes and chopped some bamboo trees down." (ANC/U.S. Army)

Although many African American women wanted to serve, only a small number were accepted because the Army was still segregated and there was a quota system that limited their number. Men could not serve as nurses at all. Without these restrictions, more nurses would have joined when they were desperately needed. Even so, by June 1942, there were twelve thousand nurses in the Army Nurse Corps.

AN ORDEAL IN THE PHILIPPINES: SURRENDER

The nurses in the jungles of Bataan could have used some of those new recruits. The two hospitals on Bataan quickly became swamped, with more patients arriving every day. At the same time, food and medical supplies were as quickly dwindling.

The jungle teemed with lizards, rats, and snakes that hung, vine-like, from trees. The heat never let up.

At Hospital #2, the patients slept outside with only the trees for shelter. "If we needed more room," says Rose Meier, "we got our axes and chopped some bamboo trees down."

In the meantime, MacArthur's American and Filipino troops were waging a courageous stand against the Japanese Army, despite suffering from malaria, dengue fever, malnutrition, and the oppressive heat.

"There were an awful lot of rumors of help coming," says Anna Williams Clark. Climbing a hill behind the hospital, she would search the harbor, looking for U.S. ships. Surely they would arrive soon with fresh troops, food, and supplies. But "there never were any ships."

As the weeks passed, supplies sank lower. Everyone—soldiers, patients, nurses, doctors—became hungrier and hungrier. By March, Rose Meier says, "We started killing the cavalry horses. And we even ate the mules."

The mess hall at Bataan's Hospital #2, where patients found plenty of benches but not much food. By March, reports one nurse, "We even ate the mules." (ANC/U.S. Army)

In the midst of this ordeal, one nurse received a late Christmas gift from home: a little black hat with a frilly veil. Dressed in her grimy coveralls, she placed it daintily on her head. The other nurses collapsed in laughter, but many were close to tears. Would they ever again see that world where they could dress up in pretty things?

Then came troubling news. General MacArthur had been ordered to leave the Philippines for Australia. "I shall return," he promised.

But what would happen to the Filipinos and Americans he left behind? Why was there no help from the United States? According to some historians, the Japanese Navy had made it virtually impossible for U.S. ships to reach the Philippines, but the troops didn't know that. They felt that the United States had abandoned them, and they were bitter, calling themselves the Battling Bastards of Bataan. The nurses were also known as BBBs: Battling Belles of Bataan.

In late March, as the fighting intensified, Hospital #1 was bombed. Two nurses were wounded, and many patients were killed.

One morning, when the air was thick with smoke and gunfire, Anna Williams Clark climbed her hill again and found U.S. and Filipino troops retreating from battle. "I'll never forget the dejection and the sadness . . . of the men as they came along," she says, ". . . covered in bandages and blood and dirt. I knew then that we were going to have to move."

On April 8, "We were told toward nightfall to grab what we could carry and get on the bus," says Hattie Brantley. The United States was surrendering Bataan to the Japanese, and the nurses were being sent to Corregidor. The nurses pleaded to stay, insisting that they could not abandon their patients, but the Army's orders were firm.

At dawn, "we got down to the beach at Mariveles," explains Anna Williams Clark, where they boarded "any kind of tiny boats" to sail to Corregidor. "There were [Japanese] planes overhead and they were strafing the boats," she adds. The sky glowed with fire as U.S. troops blew up ammunition dumps before the surrender.

Upon reaching Corregidor, the nurses were rushed into the Malinta Tunnel, where at least they had a solid roof over their heads. But they worried about the men they'd left behind. They later learned that the Japanese had marched the sixty thousand American and Filipino soldiers through scorching heat for more than seventy miles, en route to inhumane prison camps. Because the men were starving, and so many were sick, a lot of them collapsed, often prompting their Japanese captors to beat or bayonet them to death. The Bataan Death March was one of the most brutal chapters of World War II.

"I had always heard that Corregidor was terrific," says Anna Williams Clark. "They could hold out forever and they had supplies and they had everything that was necessary."

For a while, life in the Malinta Tunnel did seem bearable, if not terrific. The tunnel was hot, dusty, and humid, however. It smelled bad, like "old shoes," said one nurse. The triple-decker bunks were hopping with bedbugs.

The Japanese pounded the Rock with bombs. "Sometimes they'd hit the entrance of our tunnel and dust would get into our ventilating systems," says Bertha Henderson. "The patients and the nurses practically couldn't breathe. But we just kept working." They had to: Casualties were filling the already-crowded tunnel. Food and supplies were dwindling, just like on Bataan.

Between air raids, the nurses gulped fresh air at the tunnel entrance, where they sometimes ran into General Jonathan Wainwright. Wainwright, who now commanded the Philippine forces, was "the friendliest person on the face of the earth," recalls Rita Palmer James. He called the nurses "Angels of Bataan." His men called him "Skinny."

Poor Skinny. The Japanese had backed his troops into a corner. There was little food or water left in the tunnel, and there was no help on the way.

One night in late April, there was a rare chance to evacuate some of the nurses on two small airplanes. One plane reached Australia safely, but the other made a stop in the southern Philippines, and at takeoff, "the bottom of the plane . . . taxied onto the rocks," says Rita Palmer James. "It was just like a can opener, opening up at the bottom. We stuffed sweaters and everything else we could get in it, hoping we could get it in the air." Nothing worked. They remained on the ground, and on May 10, the nurses and the crew were taken prisoner by the Japanese.

Twelve more nurses, including a Navy nurse, managed to escape from Corregidor by submarine and reach the United States safely. But the fifty-five Army nurses who remained on Corregidor would not see the United States for a long, long time.

By May 6, General Wainwright had no choice but to surrender. His message to President Roosevelt concluded, "With profound regret and with continued pride in my gallant troops I go to meet the Japanese commander. Good-bye, Mr. President."

The nurses' fate now lay in the hands of the Japanese, whose troops had been known to rape and murder. "General Wainwright told us not to be afraid," says Rose Meier. He made it clear to the Japanese officers that the nurses were part of the medical corps and were not to be abused.

In fact, no harm came to the nurses. For more than a month

after the surrender, they cared for more than a thousand patients in the dim, dusty recesses of the tunnel, trying to make do with scarce food and medical supplies.

Then one sticky July morning, they were put on board a freighter. It sailed to Manila, where, Hattie Brantley says, "We were ordered into open trucks and there was a Japanese guard with a bayonet in each truck. We were driven through the streets of Manila to Santo Tomas."

Santo Tomas University in Manila, Luzon, Philippines. During the war, it served as an internment camp for more than three thousand Allied civilians, sixty-six Army nurses, and eleven Navy nurses. (ANC/U.S. Army)

During peacetime, Santo Tomas was a university. Now, behind its high iron gates, it was a huge internment camp for about three thousand Allied civilians, including approximately four hundred children. The two nurses from Camp John Hay, the nurses captured from the airplane, and eleven Navy nurses were also held here.

Now they were prisoners of war. At 6:30 A.M. each day, a loudspeaker awakened everyone with music. At 7:30, there was a breakfast of mush and a banana. During the day, each nurse worked for four hours in the camp hospital. After a goodnight song on the loudspeakers, it was lights out at nine.

No one was hurting the nurses. The food was adequate. But they were far from home, and they were prisoners. They had no idea how long they would be held, when they might be rescued by American troops, or if they would continue to be safe.

ALICE IN THE PACIFIC: ANTHILLS SIX FEET TALL

In 1941, Alice Weinstein was working as a surgical nurse at Beth Israel Hospital in Newark, New Jersey, when the Red Cross

called and asked if she'd be willing to join the Army Nurse Corps.

"I said, if we should ever go to war that I would certainly go," says Weinstein. Sure enough, soon after the Pearl Harbor attack,

Alice Weinstein served with the Army Nurse Corps in the southwest Pacific in World War II. Despite facing incredible heat, hungry ants, enemy fire, and malaria-carrying mosquitoes, she says, "It was a joy to take care of these poor guys who were hurt." *(Alice Weinstein)*

she became an Army nurse and volunteered for overseas service. "Come May, I was on my way."

"At two A.M., we all got on a train," she remembers, setting off with her fellow nurses from Camp Edwards, Massachusetts. "We didn't know where we were going. We knew we were going west. The train would stop at all these little towns, and the townspeople would come out with coffee, or cakes, or doughnuts."

Five days later, they arrived in San Francisco, where they were instructed to prepare to go overseas.

"The soldiers helped us roll all this stuff in our bedrolls because you couldn't take a suitcase," Weinstein says. "One of the girls decided she'd love to have a little portable Victrola. So she

Nurses line up to board the USS *West Point* in San Francisco on May 18, 1942. Because of security concerns, not a single one was told where she was going. *(ANC/U.S. Army)*

"We used to have a game," says Alice Weinstein, discussing these three-tiered bunks on the USS *West Point*. "The ones on the bottom [bunks] would have Be Kind to Whoever Was on Top Day." These nurses were from Johns Hopkins University. (ANC/U.S. Army)

bought this Victrola, and the song that had just come out in the States was 'Tangerine.' We played 'Tangerine' all across the Pacific," after leaving San Francisco on May 18, 1942.

They sailed aboard the USS *West Point,* a ship carrying more than six hundred nurses and seven thousand service-men, but, for security reasons, they weren't told where they were going.

Some nurses thought they were headed to Alaska. Or maybe Australia, an Allied country teeming with Ameri-can military bases, but a long and dangerous voyage away.

"We had all sorts of rumors of [enemy] subs," Weinstein recalls. The Navy carried out lifeboat drills so they'd know what to do if a torpedo hit. When the ship ran into storms, all that tossing around made many people seasick, but at least everyone knew that submarines rarely attacked in rough waters.

In late May, the *West Point* crossed the equator, which meant, first, that the nurses weren't going to Alaska, and second, that it was time for a Neptune party. The Navy always initiated "polly-wogs," that is, anyone who had never crossed the equator. "They'd do horrible things to these poor guys," says Weinstein. "They had to go through all sorts of slime. I can remember the smelly fish they had; it was just awful." The nurses had it easy. They had to serve cookies to the crew. Now they were Trusty Shellbacks of the Order of the Deep.

In early June, the nurses learned their destination at last when the *West Point* landed safely in Melbourne, Australia. Soon Weinstein and the other nurses of the 18th Station Hospital were on another train, traveling north to Townsville.

The weather here was searing hot. And the food took a little getting used to. "We complained about the mutton," remembers Weinstein. "Oh, gosh, it smelled bad." And sometimes, for tea, their Australian hostesses served them finger sandwiches filled with beans and spaghetti! "Our soldiers taught them how to make doughnuts and French fries," says Weinstein.

In July, Weinstein moved to Charters Towers, where "there was a place called Anthill Plains," she says. "They had

Army nurses knew how to have fun, no matter what. These nurses in Townsville, Australia, nicknamed their humble hut "Copley Plaza" after a swanky American hotel. *(ANC/U.S. Army)*

anthills that were at least six feet high. They had oodles of ants. You couldn't hang your panties and things on the line because the ants would come up there and eat them. Everything had to be packed in cans and sealed. And at night, to sleep, the legs of your cot were put in a can of kerosene and water so that the ants wouldn't climb up."

Besides caring for troops stationed at the neighboring air base, the nurses were treating wounded soldiers arriving from New Guinea.

New Guinea, a large island that sits like a small umbrella just a few hundred miles north of Australia, was a prime target for the Japanese. If they could seize control of New Guinea, then from there, they could more easily invade Australia.

At that point, though, Australia was fairly safe. But as U.S. troops began invading Pacific islands, like Guadalcanal, in August 1942, Weinstein longed to be closer to the war zone, where she felt she could be of more help. "All of us wanted to get there," she remembers, and she felt confident that she could work effectively under more difficult conditions. But the Pacific commanders, bent on protecting the nurses, were loath to even give them a chance to serve near the action. They were determined to keep them far back, away from the fighting, regardless of how valuable their services would be.

THE 48TH SURGICAL HOSPITAL: THE 48TH WADES ASHORE

As a girl in upstate New York, Helen Molony Reichert was such an avid swimmer that the lifeguards at the pool couldn't keep her out of the deep end. It's a good thing she liked the water because as a nurse with the 48th Surgical Hospital, she was going to wade through a lot of it—starting in North Africa in 1942.

The British had been fighting the Axis powers in North Africa since 1940, when Mussolini sent his troops from Libya, an Italian colony, into British-occupied Egypt. Hitler joined the fight in early 1941 by sending in his Afrika Korps to help the Italians. The fighting had gone back and forth, with each side taking the offensive, until November 4, 1942, when the British achieved their first major victory against the Germans in the Battle of El Alamein in Egypt.

Helen Molony Reichert, from Alplaus, New York, joined the Army Nurse Corps the Monday after the Pearl Harbor attack. "You make up your mind all of a sudden when somebody invades your country," she says. (Helen Molony Reichert)

Then, on November 8, 1942, the British and Americans launched an all-out push to drive off the enemy by invading North Africa at Algeria and Morocco. When they did, Reichert and the nurses of the 48th Surgical were there.

The nurses had little combat training, and many weren't expecting to face the harsh realities of war so quickly. One of them, upon leaving the United States, had insisted on bringing a separate suitcase for her makeup. Another had cooed over the cute little mess kits. Now, after a short stay in England, they were sailing into Algeria with the invasion fleet.

"About three o'clock A.M. we heard shots and guns," remembers Reichert. "We ran to the [portholes] and looked out. Of course, it was dark, but we could see the tracer bullets."

Later that morning they watched the soldiers leave the boat. Then it was the nurses' turn. "We were loaded down," says Reichert. "Gas masks, helmets, and a pack on our back with three days' supply of food." They descended a swaying iron staircase two stories high, then jumped into small boats that would take them to shore near the town of Arzew. "The waves were about six feet high," Reichert notes, "so the boats were going up and down, and we had to [jump in] fast."

When they were close to shore, the nurses had to hop out and wade through waist-deep water. They dashed across the sand to an empty beach house, which provided protection when, afterward, Reichert says, "the enemy came strafing the beach." As dusk fell, snipers fired through the windows, menacing the hospital staff through the early part of their stay in Arzew.

It took two days for their supplies to reach them. Until then, they were forced to operate their hospital without electricity or running water in filthy, smelly buildings. They had only their own rations to feed patients, and one chestful of medical supplies to treat the casualties pouring in from the field.

The nurses began to adapt quickly to war, but they had much to learn. For instance, they had no Geneva Cross to identify their hospital. "So we decided to take sixty [white] sheets and make a cross," explains Reichert, sewing them together by hand. "We found out later that a white cross identified an airfield!" A perfect target for the enemy!

Some of the male officers in their unit made it clear they thought it was ridiculous for women to work so close to combat areas. But the nurses did their best to ignore them, focusing instead on the wounded patients who needed them.

CHRISTMAS/HANUKKAH, 1942

In Arzew, Algeria, the nurses of the 48th Surgical Hospital were determined to celebrate Christmas. They decorated a fir tree with stars and candy canes cut from old plasma cans. They hand-stitched seven hundred Christmas stockings from yards of red serge left behind by French troops. With the help of a supply officer, they made four hundred pounds of peanut brittle, fudge, and taffy. Some of the men in their unit still considered the nurses a nuisance, but their patients appreciated their holiday cheer.

In the Philippines, the nurses at Santo Tomas helped to make presents for the children at the camp: jigsaw puzzles, toy trains, boats, and dolls. On Christmas Day, they set up a long table, complete with place cards, on the sunny lawn, where they enjoyed a big meal. Through the fall, they'd been working in the hospital. They had enough food, but home and freedom seemed worlds away.

In Australia, Alice Weinstein celebrated the holiday in Charters Towers. "I was the only Jewish nurse in our unit," she says, and so she didn't celebrate a traditional Hanukkah. "When Christmas came around," she says, "you always went through your things to see what you could give away as a little gift. And the cooks in the outfit didn't have a lot to work with, but they always put themselves out at the holidays."

When President Roosevelt delivered his Christmas Eve message on the radio, he said, "I give you a message of cheer." His voice was steady and reassuring. "This is a happier Christmas than last year" because the Allies were slowly gaining on the Axis powers.

"To you who serve in uniform," he said, "I also send a message of cheer—that you are in the thoughts of your families, your friends at home, and that Christmas prayers follow you wherever you may be."

FREE A MAN TO FIGHT

At the start of World War II, the only military jobs open to women were those of Army or Navy nurses. But because so many men were desperately needed for combat, each service branch soon admitted women to fill noncombat jobs. "Free a Man to Fight" became a popular slogan. Before long, thousands of women were in uniform, working for the military as parachute packers, postal workers, photographers, clerks, translators, radio operators, weather forecasters, cooks, truck drivers, typists, and mechanics, and at dozens of other jobs traditionally held by men.

☙ **WACs (Women's Army Corps)** (originally known as WAACs, for Women's Army Auxiliary Corps) More than 150,000 women, including 4,000 African Americans, served as WACs (pronounced "wax"). Thousands served overseas, many close to combat areas. The 6888th Central Postal Directory Battalion—the

Opposite page: Air WACs repair an airplane engine. Thousands of women joined the armed services during the war, often training for jobs traditionally held by men. (U.S. Army Air Forces)

only African American WAC unit to serve overseas—broke records for delivering the mail. Another group of WACs worked in New Mexico on the top-secret Manhattan Project, supporting the creation of the first atomic bomb.

✪ **WAVES (Women's Reserve of the Navy: Women Accepted for Volunteer Emergency Service)** The Navy had no trouble recruiting more than 100,000 women, who served in the United States and Hawaii, where they helped to handle the Navy's mail, communications systems, and various training tasks. And while WAVES didn't get to sail the seven seas, they did have the military's most stylish uniform, created by a famous fashion designer. The Navy did not immediately accept African American women, but once they did, they integrated them fully.

✪ **MRs (Marine Corps Women's Reserve)** The long, tough fight to take the island of Guadalcanal from the Japanese convinced the Marines that they needed women for noncombat jobs. Eager citizens quickly suggested nicknames for them like Femarines and Dainty Devil-Dogs. But the 23,000 women who served in the United States and Hawaii were proud to be known simply as Marines, or MRs (Marine Reservists). They worked as radio operators, clerks, mechanics, chemists, and more, and those who served with the Marine Corps Women's Reserve Band performed at Marine posts and hospitals and on national radio.

✪ **SPARs (Semper Paratus Always Ready)** Even the Coast Guard needed women to fill jobs ashore, releasing men for jobs at sea. SPARs worked as parachute riggers, radio technicians, storekeepers, bakers, radar operators and more. One highly trained group manned LORAN stations, top-secret navigational signal stations put into place when blackouts required the dimming of coastal beacons such as lighthouses. More than 10,000 SPARs served in the United States, Alaska, and Hawaii.

↻ WASPs (Women's Airforce Service Pilots) These highly trained pilots, numbering about 1,070, flew airplanes in the United States on noncombat jobs. They delivered and flight-tested airplanes, gave flight instruction, and flew cargo and military personnel. Thirty-eight were killed in plane crashes.

"Why can't these gals just stay home?"

Women joined the military out of a sense of duty, but not everyone appreciated their patriotism. Many servicemen felt that if these women were there to free a man to fight, then that increased their own chances of being sent into combat.

One WAC who served in the States remembers, "We had some women say to us in town, 'You took my son, husband's or brother's place.' We would just look at them like they were crazy."

Then there were the people who circulated nasty rumors, particularly about the WACs, calling them "loose" women with bad reputations. "Why can't these gals just stay home and be their own sweet little self, instead of being patriotic?" asked one man.[1]

But the women ignored the rumors and performed their jobs admirably. At war's end, they had the satisfaction of knowing they'd made a valuable contribution.

three

⟞⟞ 1943 ⟝

DANGEROUS WATERS,
DANGEROUS GROUND

By 1943, THE AXIS POWERS STILL CONTROLLED MOST OF EUROPE AND THE southwest PACIFIC, but the Allies were beginning to show their strength. In the Pacific, the Americans had held off the Japanese invasion of the island of Midway. In North Africa, the British had defeated the Germans in the Battle of El Alamein in Egypt. In Europe, Russian troops had trapped a quarter million Nazis in the Soviet city of Stalingrad. President Roosevelt was so optimistic that he boldly said he wanted nothing less than "unconditional surrender" from the Germans. That didn't mean that the Allies had an easy job in front of them. The road to victory still looked long and hard—but not impossible.

THE 95TH EVACUATION HOSPITAL:
WELCOME TO THE WAR

Through early 1943, Sally Hocutt, Pauline Sommars, and the other forty-six nurses of the 95th Evacuation Hospital marched and drilled at Camp Breckinridge, Kentucky.

Sally Hocutt

From Johnson County, North Carolina

(Sally J. Offutt)

Pauline M. Sommars

From Wadena, Minnesota

(Pauline Sommars Zupan)

NURSES of the

~ 95th ~

EVACUATION

HOSPITAL

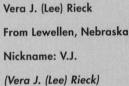

Vera J. (Lee) Rieck

From Lewellen, Nebraska

Nickname: V.J.

(Vera J. (Lee) Rieck)

Orpha Warner

From Scott City, Kansas

Nickname: Scotti

(Orpha Warner Johnson)

Marcella Korda

From Spragueville, Iowa

Nickname: Schlem

(Marcella G. Korda)

Claudine Glidewell Doyle

From Wichita, Kansas

Nickname: Speedy

(Claudine Glidewell Doyle)

Rise and shine! Nurses with the 95th Evacuation Hospital leave their tents in Oujda, French Morocco, in North Africa. (ANC/U.S. Army)

"We practiced just like the soldiers did," says Hocutt. Dressed in helmets and boots, they went for long hikes carrying full field packs. They practiced using their gas masks.

But the women had joined the Army Nurse Corps to do more than march and drill. They eagerly awaited the day they'd leave for overseas duty and begin their real work.

Finally, in April, they sailed out of New York harbor on the USS *Mariposa,* leaving the Statue of Liberty and all things American behind. Nine days later, they landed amid the exotic sights and sounds of North Africa. Just a few months earlier, this region had been alive with gunfire. But now the fighting had moved east to Tunisia, where the Allies were on the verge of defeating the Germans in North Africa.

Before landing, "they gave us so many warnings about drinking water and eating food," says Claudine Glidewell Doyle. "I had the feeling this place was pretty dirty. But it wasn't. Casablanca was beautiful. They had geraniums as big as trees."

The nurses' first home was in Oujda, French Morocco, where they lived in pyramidal tents near an olive grove. There was no running water, only a water-tank truck. "We had to wash our undies in our helmets," says Orpha Warner.

In their free time, the nurses watched the

Alice Marks of the 95th Evacuation Hospital uses her helmet, set in a rack, as a sink for washing her undies in Oujda, North Africa. (ANC/U.S. Army)

paratroopers of the 82nd Airborne and 509th Paratroopers jump from airplanes, preparing for the invasion of Italy. "Every time we'd see them," notes Vera Rieck, "we'd say, 'Well, maybe we'll get some business today,'" referring to the many broken bones they were setting.

Overall, though, the 95th Evac wasn't all that busy. There was lots of time for fun. The nurses went on picnics, played softball, and swam in the Mediterranean. The paratroopers threw parties for them, calling them their "Angels in Blue."

"From May to July, it was just one vacation for us," Rieck remembers, and the war seemed far away.

In July, the Allies invaded Sicily, and suddenly the war felt much closer. Battle casualties began arriving at the hospital's new location in Ain-el-Turck, Algeria.

"We knew that that would be a big fight over there," says Pauline Sommars. But the Allies secured

Claudine Glidewell Doyle (left) with fellow officers on the beach in Ain-el-Turck, Algeria. "We found ourselves with this beautiful beach and no bathing suits," Doyle explains. "The PX had a bunch of blue bloomers, so using those, we made the tops and skirts with white towels." (Claudine Glidewell Doyle)

Sicily so quickly that everyone felt optimistic. Better still, the Italians overthrew Mussolini and signed a peace agreement with the Allies. Things were looking so promising that the Allies felt sure they could invade mainland Italy and liberate Rome by Christmas.

But they still had to deal with the Germans, who continued to occupy the country. When the Allies invaded Italy at Salerno on

September 9, Nazi troops were ready for them. They didn't care who got caught in the crossfire, not even the nurses of the 95th Evac.

On September 10, just one day after the invasion, the nurses of the 95th Evac sailed for Salerno aboard the HMS *Newfoundland,* a British hospital ship. The men from their unit—the doctors and enlisted men—had already landed in Italy with the invasion troops.

When the *Newfoundland* arrived in the Gulf of Salerno, "there was so much gunfire on the beach," reports Sally Hocutt, that Allied commanders "wired the ship's captain. They said, please take your ship out thirty miles and cruise around."

Even so, that night, despite red and green lights identifying it as a hospital ship, the *Newfoundland* was bombed.

In a letter to her mother, Vera Rieck described what happened:

At five-ten [A.M.], we heard a plane and that God-awful whistle of a bomb make a bang. . . . I thought sure I was dying, could feel hot water flowing on my face and body, heavy boards on my chest that had fallen from the ceiling. . . . I couldn't see for the terrific smoke in our room. . . . I found [my coveralls] on the floor all soaked with water and black with dirt, put them on and found my shoes, grabbed my helmet and water canteen, and grabbed onto someone's arm and followed the light that Claudine was holding. . . . When we got on the deck, we all had to go on one side because the bomb had torn away the other side of the ship.

The American nurses, who were taken by lifeboat to a nearby ship, all survived, but several British nurses perished in the bombing.

The nurses returned to North Africa but only for a brief rest.

Soon they were on their way back to Italy to join their unit in Paestum, near Salerno.

"Oh, [the hospital was] just loaded with patients," remembers Pauline Sommars. "They couldn't get [them all] in the tents."

The bloody invasion at Salerno had left the doctors and corpsmen exhausted from treating battle casualties nonstop. They were relieved to see the nurses, who went right to work as the fighting raged just fifteen miles away. For the first time, their unit was functioning as a true evacuation hospital, one of the most forward links in the Army's system of care called the chain of evacuation. Their patients usually had already received some treatment, first from a medic or battalion aid station on the battlefield, and at a field hospital, which was generally located closer to the front than an evacuation hospital. If a patient needed additional care, he then was moved to a station hospital well away from the front, or to a large general hospital, located far from the action and perfect for recuperation or further treatment.

Because evacuation and field hospitals followed the front lines, they had to move frequently and relied on a motor section, with drivers and mechanics, to transfer them from place to place. They also needed ambulance drivers and dentists, a chaplain to tend to patients' spiritual needs, a

A doctor and ambulance driver at a military hospital in Texas *(James A. Taylor)*

mess unit to cook for them, and enlisted men to help with medical tasks and to set up tents. As they followed the front, they leapfrogged other field and evacuation hospitals. Then, when the front moved again, they stayed put as hospitals to the rear leapfrogged past them. That way, some units were always close to the battle to receive fresh casualties while other units remained behind. This allowed their patients to rest as the unit received patients requiring less urgent treatment.

The 95th Evacuation Hospital moved to Naples in October and then, around Thanksgiving, to Capua, north of Naples, where they were set up in tents. By this time, it was clear that the Allies would not reach Rome by Christmas. In fact, the Italian campaign had turned

This photograph was taken by Margaret Bourke-White, a famous photojournalist and war correspondent, who was a great admirer of the nurses. In 1943, while visiting the Italian front for a story, she stayed with nurses in a field hospital located so close to the fighting that their "beds trembled all through the night." The nurses worried not about themselves, though, but about their brothers "scattered throughout the various war theaters of the world." Army nurses "walk in beauty," Bourke-White wrote, even when their boots are caked with mud, as in this photo. (From *Purple Heart Valley: A Combat Chronicle of the War in Italy*, by Margaret Bourke-White, Simon & Schuster, N.Y., 1944.) (Photo by Margaret Bourke-White/LIFE Magazine©TIME Inc.)

into a slow and grueling slog, with a constant flow of casualties.

Amazingly, the nurses of the 95th Evac still found time to make fudge. The fudge "had to be beaten and beaten and beaten," says Orpha Warner. "Oh, we all got so tired of beating!" And if an air raid hit as the fudge cooked? "We'd get in our foxhole," says Claudine Doyle, and if anyone ventured out, the others would yell, "Stir the fudge!"

The fudge was a welcome treat in the midst of endless hard work. "When we hit Italy, we paid for that vacation we had in Africa," says Claudine Doyle. "We were taking patients from the front lines there, and forever more."

But as busy as they were now, it was just a warm-up act for what they would face in the early months of 1944.

An Army nurse wades ashore at Naples, Italy, in November 1943. *(National Archives)*

AN ORDEAL IN THE PHILIPPINES: A CAPTIVE EXISTENCE

The nurses interned at Santo Tomas had once been as busy as the nurses of the 95th Evacuation Hospital. Now, as POWs, they looked for activities to fill their days.

"Everybody had a duty," Anna Williams Clark recalls. "We had bank presidents that were garbage collectors." Elderly internees were in charge of handing out toilet paper, a few squares a day. "'Tissue issue' we called it."

The nurses were still working in the hospital four hours a day. In their free time, they played bridge or knitted. They took classes in Spanish, writing, and English literature taught by other internees.

POW nurses at Santo Tomas, photographed by their Japanese captors, in 1943. "I think the most difficult thing was not to know what was going on in the world," says Bertha Henderson, far left. "Not to receive mail from loved ones. Not to know whether our family was dead or alive, or what was happening back home." (ANC/U.S. Army)

"I read *Gone with the Wind,*" remembers Bertha Henderson. But "every time we'd start reading, people in the books were always eating or drinking. . . . You'd always think of food."

Fortunately, there was still enough to eat at Santo Tomas, though it wasn't very appetizing: cornmeal mush for breakfast, and for dinner, carabao (water buffalo) stew.

"In the beginning," says Henderson, "the Japanese did allow the Filipinos to bring in a little food." The Filipinos, who helped the internees throughout the war, set up stalls and sold fruit. Some nurses grew vegetables in little garden plots.

But the Japanese civilians who ran the camp had too many rules for the nurses to ever forget they were prisoners. They had to bow to the guards, which they found humiliating.

Then there was the waiting in line. Says Clark, "You had to line up for everything: to clean your teeth, to eat, and to shower. You had to get in line even to go to the toilet." Santo Tomas was so crowded, she adds, that the toilets were "about the only place you had any privacy at all. You were constantly with people," even in the showers.

In the nurses' dorm, the cots were so close together there was barely enough room to walk between them. Some families sought privacy by living in shanties in the courtyard.

A letter from home would have made life more bearable, but the Japanese were not delivering their mail. Says Hattie Brantley, "Every day we said, 'Help is on the way, it'll be here tomorrow.' We lived on faith and hope and trust."

Families at Santo Tomas often sought privacy by living in huts and lean-tos like these in the university courtyard. (ANC/U.S. Army)

ALICE IN THE PACIFIC: TWO HELMETS A DAY

By 1943, Alice Weinstein had left the heat and dust of northern Australia to serve in the jungles of New Guinea with the 2nd Field Hospital.

"New Guinea was very tropical and very beautiful," she remembers. The hospital was set up in a coconut grove, and the nurses lived in thatched huts. But this was no Pacific paradise, free of peril, because in New Guinea's mountainous jungles, the Allies were still fighting the Japanese. Nurses had been serving here since October 1942 and had performed so well in the face of air raids that the Army had decided to increase their presence. But the Pacific commanders were still highly protective of them. Later, as the Americans secured one Pacific island after another, the nurses who came in after the fighting ended were generally kept under armed guard and could not leave their quarters unless they were part of a group. They were subjected to evening curfews and, if they left the hospital area, had to be escorted by two armed guards.

In hot, humid New Guinea, malaria was widespread; the nurses had their hands full. For every patient who arrived with a battle wound, another four came in with malaria.

Even in the jungles of New Guinea, Army nurses took time to primp. (ANC/U.S. Army)

Malaria, carried by anopheles mosquitoes, causes fever and chills, vomiting, and headaches. In the oppressively hot New Guinea climate, the nurses had to wear long sleeves and pants to protect themselves from disease-carrying insects and had to sleep under mosquito netting.

"Because malaria was prevalent," explains Weinstein, "we had to take Atabrine, this yellow pill. And pretty soon your skin would get the color of the tablet. All of us went around looking yellow. But the natives were so enthralled with these Atabrine tablets that they used it to dye their clothes. Every native you saw was running around in something yellow."

The water in New Guinea was not safe, so the hospital staff drew their water from a Lister bag, a large canvas sack of chlorinated water that hung from

A nurse in New Guinea poses with Dug-out, the hospital mascot. (ANC/U.S. Army)

a tripod. "We were allowed two helmets full of water a day," says Weinstein. "One for washing our bodies, and one for washing our undies."

But the nurses rarely complained about such inconveniences. They were glad to be working where they were needed and eager to prove that they could perform their duties efficiently under adverse, even dangerous, conditions. Maybe, then, they could someday serve as close to the front in the Pacific theater as the nurses did in Europe.

A FLIGHT NURSE'S STORY: BEHIND ENEMY LINES

When Agnes Jensen Mangerich of Minnesota joined the Army Nurse Corps, she says, "I was anxious to see the world." A flight nurse, she treated patients evacuated by airplane from the front lines, an often dangerous job. Airplanes transporting patients often doubled as cargo planes, carrying ammunition, food, and

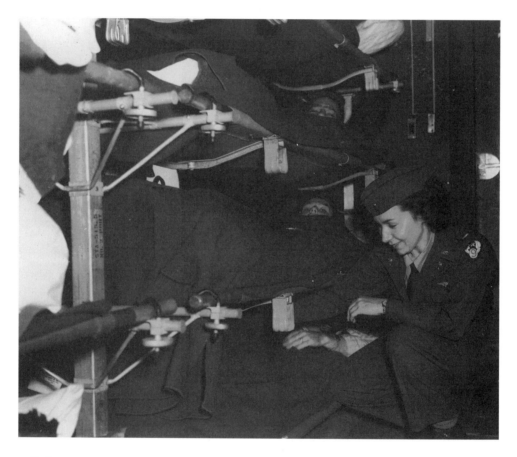

A flight nurse treats patients being evacuated by airplane. Flight nursing was especially risky because airplanes that doubled as cargo planes could not bear the protective Geneva Cross. And, of course, planes sometimes crashed. Seventeen flight nurses lost their lives in the war. (ANC/U.S. Army)

supplies, which meant they could not bear the protective Red Cross emblem. But Mangerich, undaunted, felt that "once we'd get stationed overseas, it was no more dangerous than walking across big streets in the USA. Basically, that was true—for most of them," she says.

In 1943, she arrived in Italy. Her work was fairly routine until November 8, 1943, when she boarded a plane in Sicily to pick up patients in Bari, Italy. She was joined by twelve other flight nurses and thirteen corpsmen and crew.

"We weren't very far out when we ran into very foul weather," Mangerich remembers. "We couldn't see out beyond the wing tips." Normally the trip to Bari took two hours, but as they flew for three, four hours, the nurses realized they must be lost.

When the pilot tried to land in an open field he'd spotted through the clouds, German planes swooped out of nowhere. "They shot at us," says Mangerich. "We didn't hang around. We took off."

They were lost, they'd been shot at, and they were running out of gas, but rather than panic, Agnes took a nap.

The plane was descending when she awoke, and soon they'd landed in a muddy field. When they got out of the plane, "I began to see people moving around in the bushes and the trees," she remembers. "They had guns on their backs, and a belt with ammunition."

But the strangers were friendly. One who spoke some English told them that they had landed in Albania. But he warned them that the country was occupied by Germans so they would have to escape quickly. Explaining that he and his companions were partisans, members of a Nazi-resistance party, he offered their help.

"We go to Berat," he announced.

"Right away, we said, 'How are we going to get there?'" Mangerich recalls. "And he said, 'We will walk, of course.'" And walk they did, for two and a half days before reaching Berat, where the townspeople, mistaking them for an invasion force, welcomed them with flowers and singing.

They stayed in Berat only a few days, escaping moments before the Germans came in and bombed the town. "We saw their tanks coming by, the Germans standing on the back," Mangerich says.

She and the others left in such a hurry that they were well out of town before realizing that they'd left three nurses behind. But it was too late to go back. On they walked, day after day, staying with partisan families in one village after another.

The Albanian guides led them higher and higher into the mountains. The higher they went, the poorer the villages were. The weather grew colder. Their shoes wore thin.

"The day after Thanksgiving," recalls Mangerich, "we crossed what they said was their second-highest mountain and we got caught up there in an awful blizzard. I thought sure they'd pick up our bones in the spring." The powerful wind covered their tracks immediately, and Mangerich could barely see the person ahead of her. But after nearly an hour of nothing but snow and wind, she says, "We walked out of that snowstorm just like we walked in."

That night, while staying with more partisan families, they received a message from British officers stationed in Albania, telling them how to reach them. Within days they'd arrived at their mission, where they were given shoes, medicine, and warm scarves. The British wired U.S. headquarters in Cairo, Egypt, that the Americans were there and arranged for a British guide to take them to the coast for rescue.

Led by their guide, and joined by partisans, they left the

mountains behind, walking for days toward the coast, "whether it was rain or sleet or snow or sunshine," says Mangerich. But as they drew nearer to the coast, they learned the Germans were just ahead of them.

"We went back into the mountains again," she explains. On the way, "We saw [an airfield] there that the Italians evidently had built [when Mussolini's troops occupied the country]. . . . The pilots . . . thought they could land a C-47 in there."

Messages flew over the radio. When the weather cleared, American planes would fly in and rescue them. Agnes Mangerich and the others would leave Albania the same way they arrived.

That, at least, was the plan.

CHRISTMAS/HANUKKAH, 1943

When Christmas rolled around in 1943, the nurses of the 95th Evacuation Hospital were still serving near the front lines in Capua, Italy. Not far away, Nazi troops were firing down on the Allies from a formidable hill called Monte Cassino, making it nearly impossible for them to move north to Rome.

But snow, sleet, and rain brought the fighting to a near halt, and the nurses took advantage of the lull to celebrate the holiday. They decorated a tree with balls made from rubber gloves, stuffing the hand section with old gauze and tying the fingers together, then dipping them in Epsom salts to make them sparkle. They cut angels, Santas, and stars from tin cans.

"I remember we'd walk through the wards," says Vera Rieck, "and sing Christmas songs to the patients." Some of them sang along. "A lot of them cried."

On Christmas Day, Sally Hocutt was disappointed to learn that the mess hall had run out of turkey by the time she arrived. But Richard Offutt of the 1st Armored Division cheered her up. She'd met Offutt a month before beside a bomb hole, noting, "He was a handsome young man!" He pulled out a turkey leg that he'd saved from dinner, providing them with a private Christmas feast.

In Albania, Agnes Mangerich and the other Americans spent the holiday in a little mountain town overlooking their airfield. On Christmas Eve, they got together and "sang carols and talked of Christmases past," she says. "We were all quite happy." They'd had baths and washed their hair. They'd even scrubbed away some lice. Now they were simply waiting for the weather to clear so that American planes could fly in to rescue them.

In the Philippines, the POW nurses once again made dolls and stuffed animals for the children from old clothes filled with leaves. Just before Christmas, Red Cross packages arrived for everyone in camp, each loaded with forty pounds of food, shoes, and clothes. The welcome supplies were gratifying proof that the world had not forgotten the captives of Santo Tomas.

WE WANT TO SERVE, TOO:
African American Army Nurses

If you were an African American woman who wanted to join the Army Nurse Corps in 1940, you were out of luck. Although African American nurses had served in World War I, the corps was no longer accepting them.

Mabel K. Staupers, the executive secretary of the National Association of Colored Graduate Nurses, asked President Roosevelt to help change this discriminatory policy. Soon she had the support of First Lady Eleanor Roosevelt and Dr. Mary McLeod Bethune (founder of the National Council of Negro Women and a leading champion of black education).

Thanks to their efforts, in 1941, the Army Nurse Corps began to accept African Americans. But until 1944, under the Army's quota system, they allowed only a small number to join. By war's end, only about five hundred African American women had served in the corps, but many more might have joined if they could.

At that time, because the Army was segregated, the nurses cared primarily for African American troops in the States and overseas in Africa, England, and Burma. Prudence Burns Burrell served with the 268th Station Hospital, the only African American nursing unit to go to the southwest Pacific, with service in Australia, New Guinea, and the Philippines.

"When we got up into the jungles of New Guinea," Burrell remembers, "the white hospital was down at the ocean and we were

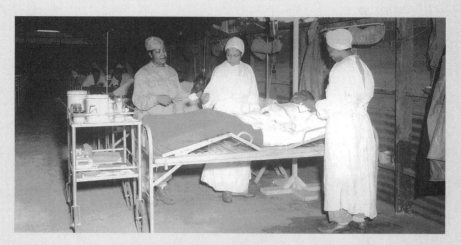

Prudence Burns Burrell, far left, served with the 268th Station Hospital, the only African American nursing unit to serve in the South Pacific. Here she assists in the surgical ward in New Guinea. *(National Archives/U.S. Army)*

farther up on the hill. The blood [supply] was labeled 'A' meaning African," she explains, because at that time, African Americans could not use white blood and vice versa.

"We had one white soldier who was there doing some building near our hospital," she continues. When he injured himself and began hemorrhaging, he hurried to them for help. "They said, 'Well, we're sorry, but our blood is labeled "A" so therefore we cannot give it to you.' And he said, 'Please, I don't [care], don't let me die.'" So they gave the "A" blood to him, saving his life.

Burrell recalls visiting a white hospital where, because of segregation, "I couldn't even go into the dining room to eat. I had to stay in the Chief Nurse's quarters."

But she has good memories, too. She laughs remembering the heavy rain in New Guinea where the nurses watched outdoor movies dressed in rain ponchos. And she married her husband, the medical administrator of the 268th Station Hospital, in the Philippines, wearing a wedding dress made from a parachute!

four

☞ 1944 ☜

"THE RAIN BEATING DOWN, THE GUNS FIRING"

BY 1944, THE ALLIES HAD ACHIEVED SOME IMPORTANT VICTORIES AGAINST the Axis powers. In the Pacific, the Marines had overwhelmed the Japanese on Guadalcanal. Now American troops were "island-hopping" closer and closer to Japan.

In Europe, the Allies had driven the Germans out of North Africa, and Russian troops were steadily chasing the Nazis out of the USSR. At some point, everyone knew, the Allies were going to invade Europe on a massive scale and aim straight for the heart of Germany. Casualties would be high, and the Army Nurse Corps, now under Superintendent Florence A. Blanchfield, prepared by initiating a new round of recruiting.

A FLIGHT NURSE'S STORY: A VERY GOOD CHOCOLATE BAR

In Albania, where Agnes Mangerich and the other Americans were awaiting rescue by airplane, the skies began to clear. But as the weather improved, the news worsened: Germans now occupied the area near their airfield, jeopardizing their escape plans.

"We got a message . . . that said planes would arrive with fighter escorts at 1300 [1:00 P.M.] the next day," says Mangerich. If it was safe for them to land, it was decided, a few of the men would signal them in with yellow parachute silk.

The next day, the Americans gathered on a small hill overlooking the airfield. Suddenly American C-47s and P-38 fighter planes swept gloriously into view. "It just seemed I could almost reach up and touch some of those P-38s," says Mangerich. They circled the field, wheels down, their pilots awaiting a flash of yellow silk.

But "we didn't signal them in," Mangerich recalls. With the Germans nearby, it was just too risky. "So they took off and left," she says. "And there we were."

There they were indeed! But the route to the coast was again clear of Germans, and on January 4, the group set off on foot once more. Within days, they'd met up with a United States officer who'd been sent in to help them.

He told them, "We're close enough to the coast, I'm sure we can make it now. But we have to go after dark. It has to be all after dark from here on."

The group had been walking since early morning. But, eager to finish their journey, they set out again at dusk and hiked all night. The next morning, they descended one last hill, and there before them lay the Adriatic Sea. They'd reached the coast at last. Soon they were munching on chocolate bars, gifts from the British who were stationed there. Says Agnes, "Oh, that candy bar was good."

By now, they'd been going for twenty-six hours straight. Exhausted, Mangerich crawled into a sleeping bag and fell fast asleep. She didn't rouse herself until late that night, and only when she learned that the rescue boat had arrived. "That got me up," she says with a laugh.

On January 9, 1944, under cover of darkness, Agnes Mangerich and the other Americans sailed quietly from Albania back to Italy. They'd spent more than two months behind enemy lines and walked more than eight hundred miles.[1]

The three nurses who were left behind in Berat didn't escape until late March. For months, partisans sheltered them from the Germans who occupied the town. They made their getaway by car, dressed as peasants and carrying fake identification cards. When they reached the coast, they sailed to safety on a torpedo boat.

THE 95TH EVACUATION HOSPITAL: "HELL'S HALF-ACRE"

The nurses of the 95th Evacuation Hospital had come a long way since the days of picnics on the beach in North Africa. They'd survived a ship bombing and a wet, exhausting autumn treating battle casualties near the Italian front. But in the early months of 1944, they faced their greatest test of courage yet in a place called Anzio.

Anzio, a coastal town just thirty-three miles south of Rome, lay in the part of Italy occupied by Germans. The Allies, unable to push past the Nazis at Monte Cassino, decided to land troops on Anzio's narrow beachhead, then beat a quick path to Rome. The invasion on January 22 completely surprised the Germans. But instead of sending the troops quickly inland, the Allies waited until more reinforcements arrived. By then, the hills overlooking the beachhead were full of Nazi troops, tanks, and guns. Soon the two sides were engaged in one of the most grueling battles of the war.

As the nurses of the 95th Evac sailed into this nightmare on January 28 aboard a tiny landing craft, they were promptly greeted by an air raid.

A nurse digs a slit trench in Anzio, Italy. The Geneva Cross on the tent was not always adequate protection from enemy fire on the beachhead. (ANC/U.S. Army)

"I looked up and my helmet fell off my head," says Claudine Doyle. "I can still see that thing filling with water and sinking. Boy, do you feel bare!"

In fact, the nurses felt pretty bare their entire stay at Anzio. The hospital area, home to several units, notes Pauline Sommars, "was kind of out in the open."

The hundreds of tents sat smack in the middle of unprotected terrain and were surrounded by enemy targets, like an airfield and a gasoline dump. The sounds of battle were almost constant.

"It was rumble, roar, day and night," remembers Vera Rieck. "They had what you called 'Screaming Meenies.'"

"There was a big gun, Anzio Annie, that they'd pull out of the mountain," explains Sommars. "A big gun on railroad tracks. At night especially, it'd be enough to wake you up."

"We learned to keep that old helmet handy," says Rieck.

The nurses often slept in foxholes dug in their tents, fully dressed. But Sally Hocutt and her tentmates hated shivering alone in these trenches, so, at their request, two enlisted men "dug our foxholes way deep so two people could fit in there," she says.

Before long the tents were riddled with holes from shrapnel. The hospital area was so dangerous, says Claudine Doyle, "the patients wouldn't stay there. They called it Hell's Half-Acre."

Then came February 7. The wards were operating at full capacity; ambulances were pulling up, loaded with wounded men. Claudine Doyle was with a patient when a doctor came in. "Speedy, here's your mail," he said, waving her to a stool. "You sit there and look at it." Suddenly, she says, "I just turned a somersault off that stool. You could hear what sounded like hail. An officer yelled, 'Put on your helmet! That was a bomb!'"

"It sounded just like thunder," says Sommars. "The tent seemed like it was going to go right up in the air."

Sally Hocutt explains what happened. "This young German

Nurses' quarters, 95th Evacuation Hospital, Anzio, Italy, 1944 *(Vera J. (Lee) Rieck)*

Claudine Glidewell Doyle snapped this photo of her tentmates soon after arriving in Anzio, Italy. They turned in surprise when a shell exploded nearby, a hint of things to come. After that, says Doyle, "I didn't take any more pictures." *(Claudine Glidewell Doyle)*

pilot had been bombing the beachside, and our Spitfires [fighter planes] took off after him. . . . He had to drop [his load of bombs] in order to escape. . . . He realized there was a hospital there; he saw the big red cross. However, he tried to miss the hospital and really did hit only the edge of it. If he'd hit dead center, he'd have killed everybody."

Marcella Korda rushed to the battered hospital. "Some of the tents looked like a sieve. We didn't know how many people had been killed."

Sommars, who'd been working near the bombed tent, says, "I could see there was a stretcher over aways." Sticking out from beneath the blanket "was a pair of nurses' shoes."

Chief nurse Blanche Sigman, assistant chief nurse Carrie Sheetz, and nurse Marjorie Morrow had been killed instantly. A Red Cross worker, Esther Richards, was also killed, as were the two enlisted men who'd dug the big foxhole in Sally Hocutt's tent. Altogether twenty-six people were killed; sixty-four were wounded, including two more nurses.

After the bombing, explains Korda, "We couldn't function as a hospital because we'd lost quite a few personnel and all of our x-ray equipment had been destroyed." The 95th Evac left Anzio a few days later but not before the area was bombed again, killing two more nurses from another unit.

The deaths so alarmed the Army that they considered withdrawing the remaining 150 nurses serving at Anzio. But they realized that the nurses were doing essential work, and as long as they were there, the troops knew that Anzio was not a lost cause. In the end, the Army relented, and the nurses stayed on.

The battle for Anzio continued through the grim, soggy winter into the spring. Roses bloomed among the rubble. To the south, the Allies finally pushed past Monte Cassino, and in May, the troops broke free from the narrow Anzio beachhead.

On June 5, President Roosevelt was able to announce on the radio, "My friends. Yesterday on June 4, 1944, Rome fell to American and Allied troops."

What he didn't reveal was that the largest Allied invasion of the war was about to begin.

THE 128TH EVACUATION AND 51ST FIELD HOSPITALS: D DAY, JUNE 6, 1944

In the spring of 1944, "England was full of Americans," says Helen Molony Reichert of the 48th Surgical Hospital—now called the 128th Evacuation Hospital. The country was covered with acres of tanks, aircraft, jeeps, and supplies, all in preparation for the invasion.

"Everybody knew we were going to invade," she says. "But we didn't know where exactly." The Germans had fortified the entire northern and western coasts of France with a gauntlet of mines, concrete barriers, and barbed wire called the Atlantic Wall. As for when the invasion would take place, again, few people knew for sure.

In the meantime, everyone was doing their part to get ready, including the nurses of the 128th Evac. "We were seasoned troops by then," Reichert says, not the inexperienced nurses who had sewn a Geneva Cross from white sheets in North Africa! Now they were in England to train the staffs of new hospital units arriving from the United States. Once the invasion began, the new units would have to be ready to spring into action.

On the night of June 5, the sky over southern England filled with hundreds of planes. Five thousand boats loaded with U.S., British, and Canadian troops set sail across the choppy waters of the English Channel, bound for the beaches of Normandy in northwestern France. Thousands of paratroopers landed ahead of them, including members of the 82nd Airborne, the ones who, in North Africa, had called the nurses their "Angels in Blue."

The invasion had begun.

June 6 was D day. Early that morning, Allied troops landed on the beaches of Normandy, which had been code-named Omaha, Utah, Sword, Gold, and Juno. The soldiers waded ashore from landing craft, many under intense enemy fire. The American invasion at Utah Beach went well, but the landing at Omaha Beach was a near disaster as well-trained German troops fired on the Americans from tall cliffs towering over the sand. By evening, D day casualties numbered in the thousands. But every beach was secured that day.

American troops aboard LCIs (landing craft infantry) draw near Omaha Beach, on France's Normandy coast, on D day, June 6, 1944. The Normandy invasion was the largest amphibious invasion in history. *(National Archives/U.S. Navy)*

The first Army nurses to care for D day casualties were those of the 12th and 13th Hospital Train Units—but they didn't reach Normandy by train. Sailing on two British hospital ships, they arrived off Omaha Beach on June 7 and Utah Beach on June 8, and began caring for the wounded before they were evacuated back to England.

On June 10, long before things had settled down, the nurses of the 128th Evacuation Hospital arrived on Utah Beach. They'd left England the day before, dressed in fatigues. "We didn't take off those clothes for a long time!" Helen Reichert remembers with a laugh.

At dawn, as her ship neared the Normandy shore, Reichert went up on deck to use the bathroom. "This glider [bomb] came down . . . and it fell in between our ship and the ship that was next to us and exploded," she says. "It blew in part of our ship."

The nurses sailed to shore on small landing boats, then waded through the water and ran across the beach to safety. The soldiers had laid down a metal track on the sand for tanks and other heavy vehicles, part of the elaborate D day preparations. Says Reichert, "I looked down and I said, well, this is nice. It was an improvement over our Arzew beach."

Helen Dixon Johnson, a nurse from California, landed on Omaha Beach two weeks after D day. Even then, she remembers, "There was debris all over: tanks and trucks and parts of equipment, machine guns, everything. There were [barrage] balloons all over," large balloons that hovered over the water to help protect ships against air attacks.

Nurses on Omaha Beach take time out for a bite to eat. Nurses began arriving on the Normandy beaches just four days after D day. (ANC/U.S. Army)

The ack-ack (antiaircraft fire) was so loud, she says, "you could hardly hear yourself think." On shore, signs such as one saying "Roads Cleared of Mines to the Hedge" directed them to safe paths. Before the invasion, the enemy had littered the coast with mines, explosive devices usually laid underwater or just below the ground that can kill or maim people and destroy ships, tanks, and other equipment when run over or stepped on.

Johnson, a member of the 3rd Auxiliary Surgical Unit, was assigned to the 51st Field Hospital near the town of Saint-Lô, close to the front lines. She worked at least twelve hours a day, usually more. Cows, abandoned by their owners, followed the nurses, hoping to be milked, bees swarmed the canned peaches in their K-rations, and enemy

Helen Dixon Johnson of California arrived on Omaha Beach just two weeks after D day. *(Helen Dixon Johnson)*

fire was never far away. One night the Germans bombed the hospital area, and the nurses jumped into slit trenches. "They were all full of this garbage," says Johnson, but "we didn't care."

The Allies had hoped to move quickly inland after the invasion, but they were having a terrible time pushing past the Germans, who had taken cover behind Normandy's tall, thick hedgerows. Finally, in late July, the frustrated Allies launched a massive air attack near Saint-Lô, and the German lines began to crumble.

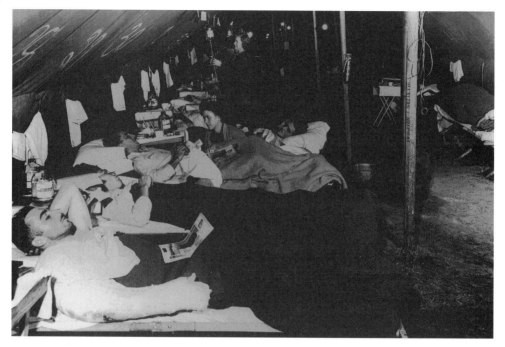

A nurse tends her patients in a field hospital in France, 1944. *(ANC/U.S. Army)*

When Helen Johnson's unit traveled through Saint-Lô, "it was pulverized," she notes. "The only thing we found was an old man and a seven-year-old boy, and one chicken we couldn't catch. Dead Germans and dead horses littered the streets."

Now the Allies were in the clear. They moved swiftly eastward, liberating one French town after another in their push toward Germany. On August 25, they answered every Frenchman's prayer by liberating Paris.

The grateful Parisians greeted the Allies as heroes. Maureen Martin, a nurse with the 128th Evacuation Hospital, visited Paris soon after the liberation. The Parisians thought the nurses in their combat clothes were truck drivers, but "they were very kind to us," she says. A young man offered to show them the city, taking them to the Arc de Triomphe, the Eiffel Tower, and the Church of the

Maureen Martin, from Bellefontaine, Ohio, served with the 128th Evacuation Hospital. While stationed in France, she attended Bing Crosby's touring USO show. "There must have been several thousand men [there], but there were twenty nurses in our group," she says. As the women made their way through the sea of soldiers, she recalls, "Someone in the crowd all of a sudden yelled, 'Look at the nurses!' And with that, everybody in that field stood up and gave us a standing ovation." (Maureen J. Martin)

Dome in the Hôtel des Invalides, home of Napoléon's Tomb. The church's gilded dome had just been cleaned, and Martin remembers, "It just shone like gold."

THE 95TH EVACUATION HOSPITAL:
BONJOUR, FRANCE!

Since leaving Anzio, the nurses of the 95th Evac had been serving elsewhere in Italy, even relaxing, playing softball, and sight-seeing in Rome. But on August 15, the Allies invaded southern France, and the nurses of the 95th Evac came in right behind them, landing at Saint-Tropez just four days after the troops. This time their landing was uneventful, and they soon joined the men in their unit near the town of Gonfaron.

But the front was moving so fast that they didn't stay long; the hospital moved frequently to keep up with the troops. They traveled through lovely mountain country where "they had these beautiful grape vineyards," remembers Vera Rieck.

The French welcomed "Les Libérateurs" with eggs, chickens, rabbits, and ducks. "When we were set up at Saint-Amour," remembers Marcella Korda, "we were invited to the home of French people." She can't recall the whole menu, but "one thing I do remember is French onion soup and it was absolutely delicious."

Pauline Sommars's roommate, on the other hand, wound up with a gift of cheese. Says Sommars, "It was some real smelly cheese!"

In mid-September the Allied troops coming from southern France met up with the Allied forces in the north, forming one broad line advancing on Germany. But the fall brought rain, mud,

French mud *(Pauline Sommars)*

and more casualties. The front bogged down; the advance slowed. Still, on December 15, in Mutzig, France, the 95th Evac found something to celebrate: Sally Hocutt married Richard Offutt, the nice young man she'd met beside the bomb hole in Italy.

Sally and Richard Offutt on their wedding day in Mutzig, France. The town's mayor ordered citizens to donate eggs for their wedding cake so the cooks wouldn't have to use powdered eggs. *(Sally J. Offutt)*

"It was a formal wedding," Hocutt explains. "My dear Aunt Ruth sent me a white wedding gown and dresses for the bridesmaids." When she went to mail them, the postmaster in Raleigh, North Carolina, told her she was crazy; the dresses would never make it to the war zone! But, says Sally, her aunt told him, "'You send them. My niece Sally asked for them and she will certainly receive them.' Sure enough, they came through."

Vera Rieck was one of three bridesmaids, and Colonel Paul K. Sauer, the unit's chief surgeon, gave Hocutt away.

That year in his annual report, Sauer wrote, "The nurses have stood out as magnificent examples of courage and devotion to duty." Despite all they'd been through, he continued, "their sense of good sportsmanship and good humor never left them. Are women really the weaker sex?"

THE 128TH EVACUATION AND THE 51ST FIELD HOSPITALS: THE BATTLE OF THE BULGE

After leaving Normandy, Helen Dixon Johnson and the nurses of the 51st Field Hospital moved frequently as their unit tried to keep up with the swiftly advancing front line. Over and over again, they encountered grateful French citizens. Johnson remembers one old lady who "was so thankful that the Americans had come that she gave me this game hen and two bags of feed. Well, I accepted it, but I thought, what am I going to do with it?" She kept it as a pet until it started waking everyone up at the crack of dawn. "So I gave it to a little boy in Belgium," she says, when the hospital reached there in September. Soon after that, they followed the troops into Germany.

The nurses of the 110th Evacuation Hospital, bathing here in a Belgian stream. They knew little German, so when caring for German POWs, they sometimes instructed them to "Sittenzee up!" or "Rollenzee over!" (ANC/U.S. Army)

As fall set in, though, the Allied advance slowed. The front lines had moved too fast for supplies to reach them, and the weather was miserable. The muddy conditions made progress difficult. "At Aachen, [Germany]," says Johnson, "it rained and rained and rained. We had maybe two or three inches of mud on the operating room floor."

At the 128th Evacuation Hospital, not far from Aachen,

"we were sitting in fields of mud," says Maureen Martin. They were also treating German POWs. "We were taught to treat the POWs just as we would treat the other patients," she says, as dictated by the Geneva Conventions.

Despite the bad weather and the slow advance, the Allies were optimistic. "We thought that [the war] was almost over," remembers Helen Johnson. "Then everything let loose."

The Allied front that stretched along the western edge of Germany was strong and well manned in all but one spot: the Ardennes Forest in Belgium. In 1940, Nazi tanks had smashed through this very spot to capture France, and on the cold, foggy morning of December 16, 1944, Hitler ordered a major attack on the American troops there. He believed that if he could split the Allied front line in two, Germany could still win the war.

U.S. soldiers move through a snowy forest during the Battle of the Bulge. *(National Archives/U.S. Army)*

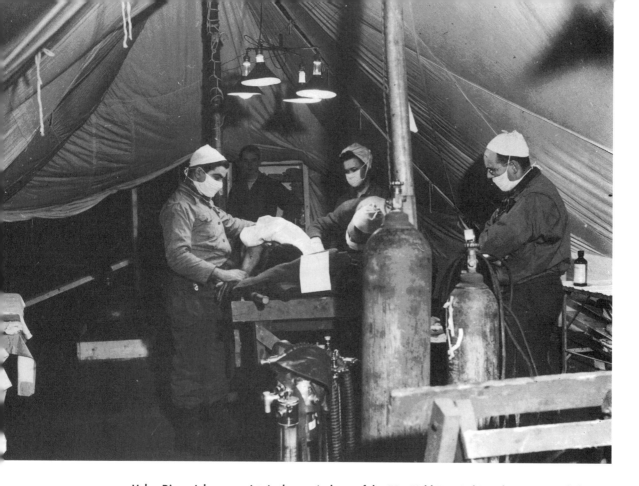

Helen Dixon Johnson assists in the surgical tent of the 51st Field Hospital in Belgium. Located close to the front lines, the 51st once handled more than a thousand patients in a sixty-three-hour period. (ANC/U.S. Army)

The surprise attack wreaked havoc in the Allied lines. Hospitals hastily shut down to move to safer areas; the 51st Field Hospital relocated from Germany to Huy, Belgium.

"We were set up in a field of snow," remembers Helen Johnson. It was so cold that engineers had to use special drills to drive the tent poles into the ground. The potbellied stoves in the tents couldn't provide enough heat. "The I.V. fluids were too cold to flow," she notes.

The Germans tore through the Allied front, creating a "bulge," or gap, in the lines. They surrounded American troops in the Belgian town of Bastogne, but the Americans refused to surrender.

A medic pulls a litter through the snow in Belgium. *(National Archives/U.S. Army)*

The nurses, in the meantime, were busy caring for the onslaught of casualties. In addition to the wounded, thousands of soldiers were admitted for trench foot. This condition, common among men serving in the wintry trenches, came from never removing their wet, cold boots. Johnson, a surgical nurse, was on duty twelve to sixteen hours a day. "It was mostly just work, work, work," she says.

Eventually, the American forces prevailed. During the Battle of the Bulge, which ended in January, more than twelve thousand Germans were killed. They'd lost more equipment than they could replace. Never again would they be strong enough to launch such a large-scale attack.

ALICE IN THE PACIFIC: TO TACLOBAN

In late October 1944, Alice Weinstein had left New Guinea and was sailing aboard the *John Alden.*

"We hear there are twenty-seven females on their way to the Philippines," Tokyo Rose said on the ship's radio. "Oh, girls, I feel so sorry for you, you'll never get there. I hope you realize how terrible your parents are going to feel."

Tokyo Rose, a female disc jockey who worked for the Japanese, was talking about Weinstein and the other nurses on board. Of course, Tokyo Rose couldn't be trusted; her American-style radio shows were intended to lower the morale of American troops by making them yearn for home. But she was right, there *were* twenty-seven nurses on board the *John Alden,* and they *were* going to the Philippines. If she knew that much, how much more might she know?

The nurses knew theirs was a dangerous mission. U.S. troops, under General MacArthur, were about to invade the Philippines. Because so many casualties were expected, the surgeon general had insisted that nurses be allowed to participate early on, and for once, the Pacific commanders had agreed. Now Alice Weinstein and the nurses of the 1st and 2nd Field Hospitals were on their way, accompanied by Lieutenant Colonel Nola Forrest, the director of nurses for the southwest Pacific.

As they drew near the Philippine island of Leyte, the naval Battle of Leyte Gulf was winding down.

"They had all those kamikaze pilots coming down," remembers Weinstein. Japanese kamikaze pilots flew their planes, loaded with explosives, directly into a ship, blowing it up and committing suicide at the same time.

"Then they announced this typhoon was coming in," Colonel Forrest says, and soon it hit with ninety-mile-per-hour winds.

On November 1, contrary to Tokyo Rose's prediction, the *John Alden* docked at Tacloban on Leyte. "They put us on these trucks and took us to a cathedral where we were going to have our hospital," says Weinstein. Within three hours of reaching the cathedral, the nurses were treating six hundred patients.

"You'd end up with two nurses taking care of one hundred patients," Weinstein says. But "you just felt so fortunate to be all in one piece when you'd look at some of these poor patients that you just went ahead and did it."

This cathedral in Leyte, in the Philippines, served as a hospital after the invasion while continuing to offer religious services. Morning mass was conducted as the nurses served their patients breakfast, and the hospital staff used the baptismal bowl for scrubbing up. *(Hulton-Deutsch Collection/Corbis)*

October marked the beginning of the rainy season, and that month, Leyte received twice the normal rainfall. The nurses got used to tromping through mud. Mud couldn't hurt them, but enemy fire was another story.

"For a couple of nights they made us stay in the cathedral," Forrest says. "One night [the Japanese] came over about twenty times. A lot of us slept on the altar floor. My head was under the bishop's chair."

75

One day, as Colonel Forrest was working in a tent with the flaps open, a Japanese pilot flew straight at the tent and fired into it. The shot missed, but, Colonel Forrest says, "I can still see his face. He was that close."

The nurses were living with a Filipino family in a house built on stilts, with the family's carabao stabled in the space underneath.

"They had these big milk cans and those were our johns," Alice Weinstein says. The nurses had a rack to hold their helmets for washing, and they were allotted the usual two helmets of water a day. If there was an air raid while they were washing up, "Zip! There went your water!" she says, laughing. "You had to put the helmet on your head!"

It was more than a month before additional nurses arrived on Leyte. By the end of 1944, more than five hundred nurses were working in island hospitals.

In the meantime, Alice Weinstein and the other nurses had proved that, even in the Pacific war zone, nurses could perform their work with courage and efficiency.

AN ORDEAL IN THE PHILIPPINES: SLOW HUNGER

This had been the Santo Tomas POWs' toughest year yet. Japanese military commanders had assumed control of the camp, and they were much stricter than their civilian predecessors. At night, soldiers brandishing bayonets patrolled the university, which was now lit up like a prison with harsh electric lights.

The Japanese no longer allowed the Filipinos into the camp to sell fresh fruits and vegetables. They "became stricter and stricter," says Bertha Henderson, and, of course, the food got scarcer and scarcer. "They didn't have enough food to feed their own forces." Now meals consisted of rice and corn, with an occasional dose of soybeans or dried salted fish. The food shortage reflected just how badly things were going for the Japanese. Back in Japan, their own people were hungry, too.

Says Anna Williams Clark, "One of the best pastimes in camp was trading recipes. Patients would sit there with swollen feet from beriberi and scurvy and all the rest of it. They'd be discussing foods and collecting recipes. We wrote up recipe books."

Internees were beginning to die from starvation. Many suffered from tuberculosis, but the nurses lacked adequate medicines to treat them. "We continued to do what we were trained to do," says Helen Nestor. "I think that was part of our salvation. The more time we had to think of somebody else . . . the less we had to cry in our own beards."

The nurses, as hungry as everyone else, lived on rumors that help was coming. But most of the talk amounted to nothing.

Then, in September, they heard the drone of approaching airplanes. Suddenly they were flying overhead, and they were *American* planes! As bombs dropped in the distance, the prisoners' hopes soared. Surely, rescue was only days away.

"That night, they played 'Pennies from Heaven' [over the loudspeaker]," remembers Bertha Henderson. "That gave us a big morale boost."

"Then, for quite a period of time, two or three weeks," notes Helen Nestor, "there was nothing. We couldn't hear a thing in the distance. No more air raids or anything." Now the song on the loudspeaker was "Lover Come Back to Me." The Japanese cut back on rations even more, which led to increased hunger and more deaths.

Then in October, hopes soared again as the air raids resumed. One night, the commentator on the loudspeaker signed off by saying, "Better Leyte than never." Somehow he knew that MacArthur's troops had landed in the southern Philippines.

Says Helen Nestor, "From the first air raid, we knew the time had come for us. Then it was a case of hanging on 'til they came."

CHRISTMAS/HANUKKAH, 1944

In 1944, the nurses at Santo Tomas barely tried to celebrate the holiday. Everyone was too hungry. They had no materials left to make toys for the children. The children thought it might be better if Santa Claus didn't come because he might be spotted by the searchlights and killed by antiaircraft fire.

Santa didn't visit Santo Tomas on Christmas Eve, but American planes did. They dropped leaflets all over Manila that read, "The American Forces of Liberation wish . . . the people of the Philippines all the blessings of Christmas and the realization of their fervent hopes for the New Year."

The nurses' most fervent hope, of course, was for rescue. At the rate that people were dying, the Americans could not come soon enough.

In Europe, the Battle of the Bulge forced the 128th Evacuation Hospital to move from Brand, Germany, to Verviers, Belgium. Says Maureen Martin, "We had all planned dates with the fellow we were going with in other units. Of course, we moved . . . and they had no idea where we were so there went our Christmas plans."

On Christmas Day, the hospital started admitting patients straight from the battlefield as enemy planes and buzz bombs flew overhead.

The nurses of the 128th Evac had now been through four wartime Christmases, three of them spent overseas. They wondered if they would celebrate Christmas 1945 in a tent hospital close to the front lines or back home in the USA.

When the 128th Evacuation Hospital was set up in this school building in Verviers, Belgium, the staff saw German buzz bombs fly overhead almost every day. The bombs were actually unmanned planes, loaded with explosives, headed for England. "When we were still in the tents," says Maureen Martin, "we were in what we called Buzz Bomb Alley." Buzz bombs made an eerie putt-putt sound, and "some of them were so low that they would make the tent flaps weave," she recalls. *(Maureen J. Martin)*

FRANCES SLANGER:

"And me with a flashlight, writing..."

On October 21, 1944, Army nurse Frances Slanger wrote the following letter to *The Stars and Stripes* newspaper while stationed near the Belgian-German border. Her letter expressed the feelings of Army nurses everywhere. Less than twenty-four hours later, Slanger was dead, killed by a German shell, making her the first nurse to die by enemy fire in the European theater.

It is 0200 [2:00 A.M.] and I have been lying awake for one hour, listening to the steady, even breathing of the other three nurses in the tent.... The rain is beating down on the tent with torrential force.... The wind is on a mad rampage and its main objective seems to be to lift the tent off its poles and fling it about our heads.

The fire is burning low and just a few live coals are on the bottom.... I couldn't help thinking how similar to a human being a fire is; if it is allowed to run down too low and if there is a spark of life left in it, it can be nursed back.... So can a human being. It is slow, it is gradual, it is done all the time in these Field Hospitals and other hospitals in the ETO.

We had read several articles in different magazines and papers sent in by a grateful GI, praising the work of the nurses around the combat areas. Praising us—for what?

... The GI's say we rough it...

We wade ankle deep in mud. You have to lie in it. . . . We have a stove and coal. We even have a laundry line in the tent. Our GI drawers are at this moment doing the dance of the pants what with the wind howling, the tent waving precariously, the rain beating down, the guns firing, and me with a flashlight, writing. It all adds up to a feeling of unrealness.

Sure we rough it, but in comparison to the way you men are taking it, we can't complain, nor do we feel that bouquets are due us. But you, the men behind the guns, the men driving our tanks, flying our planes, sailing our ships, building bridges . . . it is to you we doff our helmets. To every GI wearing the American uniform, for you we have the greatest admiration and respect. . . .

. . . We have learned a great deal about our American soldier and the stuff he is made of. The wounded do not cry. Their buddies come first. The patience and determination they show, the courage and fortitude they have is sometimes awesome to behold. It is we who are proud to be here. Rough it? No. It is a privilege to be able to receive you and a great distinction to see you open your eyes and with that swell American grin, say "Hi-ya Babe!"

2d Lt. Frances Slanger,
2d Lt. Christine Cox,
2d Lt. Margaret M. Bowler,
1st Lt. Elizabeth F. Powers,
Army Nurse Corps,
in *The Stars & Stripes,* European Edition.

five

═ 1945 ═
"A CREDIT TO MY COUNTRY"

*"I shall endeavor to be a credit to my Country
and to the uniform I wear."*

—Pledge of the Army Nurse

BY 1945, THE NEED FOR MILITARY NURSES WAS SO GREAT THAT PRESIDENT Roosevelt proposed that they be drafted. Great Britain, after all, had been drafting women into service since 1941. The U.S. House of Representatives did pass legislation to draft nurses, but things happened so fast in 1945 that it never had time to become law.

The end of the war in Europe appeared to be so near that in February, President Roosevelt met with Churchill and the USSR's Joseph Stalin in Yalta, in the USSR, to discuss the postwar future of Germany and other European countries.

Opposite page: By 1945, the need for military nurses was so dire that President Roosevelt suggested they be drafted, and the Army Nurse Corps raised its age limit from forty to forty-five years old. *(National Archives)*

Nurses Are Needed Now!

FOR SERVICE IN THE

ARMY NURSE CORPS

IF YOU ARE A REGISTERED NURSE AND NOT YET 45 YEARS OF AGE
APPLY TO THE SURGEON GENERAL, UNITED STATES ARMY,
WASHINGTON 25, D. C., OR TO ANY RED CROSS PROCUREMENT OFFICE

AN ORDEAL IN THE PHILIPPINES: FREEDOM

By February, the nurses at Santo Tomas knew that American troops were nearby. Machine guns rattled to the north of Manila. Fires blazed throughout the city, filling the sky with billows of smoke. Then an American pilot flying overhead tossed out his goggles with a message attached that read, "Cheer up. Christmas is coming, today or tomorrow."

The Japanese commanders knew the Americans were close, too, and they were prepared. They "set up their machine gun nests right there on the campus," says Helen Nestor. They dug foxholes and brought in guns and ammunition.

On the evening of February 3, "We were all ordered into the main building," says Bertha Henderson. "We were told not to leave . . . under any circumstances."

Through the dusk, they heard something huge and clanking rumbling toward the camp. "Then we saw some searchlights," says Henderson. "We could smell gasoline." Suddenly American tanks were crashing through the gates of Santo Tomas.

"We heard someone yell, 'Are there Americans in there?'" says Helen Nestor. "And it seems as though the whole education building, it was like in one voice, replied, 'You'd better believe it!'"

Fighting broke out between the GIs and the Japanese, and the nurses stepped right in to tend the wounded. The GIs looked "like giants," said one nurse, compared to the starving internees. They "gave us some of their chocolate, which tasted like heaven," says Anna Williams Clark. They gave them their rations.

"The next day," says Bertha Henderson, "they raised our flag in front of the building and someone started singing 'God Bless America.' Of course it was just the most wonderful feeling."

But Santo Tomas was not liberated without further fighting. At one point, the Japanese "very nearly retook the camp," says Rita Palmer James. "Many internees who had survived those years were killed at the end when the Japanese shelled the camp."

In the midst of the shelling, Lieutenant Colonel Nola Forrest arrived with a hundred nurses to relieve the POWs and escort them home. The POW nurses worked side by side with the new nurses treating battle casualties while Colonel Forrest made arrangements for their trip.

Lieutenant Colonel Nola Forrest was director of nurses for the southwest Pacific during the last years of the war. In New Guinea, she met Irving Berlin, composer of "God Bless America" and other popular tunes, when he was there entertaining the troops with his touring show, "This Is the Army."

"What do you dislike most about Army life?" he asked her.

"I think it's these pants," she replied. They were made of heavy twill and worn with leggings and high shoes as protection from mosquitoes.

Her reply inspired him to write this song:

OH, FOR A DRESS AGAIN
TO CARESS AGAIN—IN A DRESS AGAIN.
COVERED UP FROM HEAD TO YOUR TOE.
WE MUST HIDE WHAT WE'D LIKE TO SHOW.
OH, FOR A SKIRT AGAIN.

JUST TO FLIRT AGAIN—IN A SKIRT AGAIN.
THERE'S NO ROMANCE WHEN YOU DANCE
CHEEK TO CHEEK AND PANTS AND PANTS.
OH, FOR AN OLD-FASHIONED DRESS.

∽○∽

(Some of these lyrics later appeared in his song "Oh, To Be Home Again.") *(ANC/U.S. Army)*

Lieutenant Colonel Nola Forrest, director of nurses for the southwest Pacific, distributes orders to the newly released POWs, shown here in their brand-new uniforms. (ANC/U.S. Army)

The nurses at Santo Tomas must have dreamed of this moment when, liberated at last, they were leaving the camp by truck to board a waiting airplane. (ANC/U.S. Army)

"I had to send one nurse up to New Guinea to get uniforms for them," she says, since they'd been wearing the same clothes since 1942. There were medals to award, orders to distribute. The nurses, for their part, had a lot of catching up to do. What was all this talk about "wax"? They had never heard of WACs! And what was this penicillin the doctors were using? This antibiotic, a wonder drug discovered just before the war, was being used to treat everything from tuberculosis to infected wounds.

On February 12, the sixty-six nurses piled into trucks. For the first time in almost three years, they passed through the big front gates of Santo Tomas. They boarded a plane awaiting them on Dewey Boulevard and soon left Manila far behind.

Later, in Honolulu, Hawaii, "We all kissed the ground," says Bertha Henderson. "We had tub baths and we had a permanent and somebody found silk stockings for us."

And, of course, they ate, wolfing down steak, and ice cream, whatever they wanted. In late February, they arrived in San Francisco, home at last.

Not a single Army nurse died in Santo Tomas, which they believe was because they were able to keep working. They had survived the grim, desperate days in the jungles of Bataan, the tense weeks in the dust and grime of the Malinta Tunnel, and years of captivity and hunger at Santo Tomas.

Now, says Henderson, "All I wanted was peace and quiet. I just wanted to go back to a normal life."

Freed POW nurses ready for takeoff from the Philippines. "Our first stop was in Saipan," says Bertha Henderson. "And I remember seeing someone with a red apple. We just wept with joy, seeing a piece of fruit." (ANC/U.S. Army)

Released at last from Santo Tomas, nurses dip into their first ice cream in three years. Rita Palmer James, far left, dropped from 120 to 80 pounds during her captivity. (ANC/U.S. Army)

THE 51ST FIELD HOSPITAL:
INTO THE LAND OF THE ENEMY

On March 13, 1945, Helen Dixon Johnson and the nurses of the 51st Field Hospital made history by becoming the first Army nurses to cross Germany's Rhine River. Just days before, Allied troops had breached this last major obstacle to Germany's heartland, crossing at the town of Remagen. Now, set up in a large house, the 51st Field Hospital was serving deep in the land of the enemy.

The operating room, says Johnson, "was a dining room that looked out over the river. You could see dead horses [and] dead bodies float down."

As more and more Allied troops crossed the Rhine, so did more nurses. But the Germans were none too happy to see Americans. Children threw rocks at ambulances. The country, strained by the war's demands, was in terrible shape. Allied air attacks had crushed much of Berlin, Dresden, and other cities.

Johnson remembers the refugees, "clogging the roads with all their materials on wheels of some kind: a cart, or a baby buggy." And she can't forget the old man and woman plowing a field. "She was the horse," says Johnson, pulling the plow as the old man followed behind.

The Allies felt hopeful. Germany was too battered to fight much longer; the war had to end soon. Spring was in the air; the forsythia was in bloom.

Then, on April 12, terrible news: President Roosevelt was dead. "Everybody just felt lost," says Johnson. "They felt that the world had caved in, what were we going to do? And then Truman took over." Harry S. Truman became the nation's thirty-third president.

Harry S. Truman takes the oath of office as thirty-third president of the United States, with his wife, Bess, and daughter, Margaret, by his side. *(Harry S. Truman Library)*

In late April, American troops advancing into Germany from the west linked up with Russian soldiers coming from the east at the Elbe River. "We weren't supposed to fraternize with them," Johnson explains, but "some of our doctors were of Russian extraction and could speak [the language] so of course they were right in there and the vodka flowed very freely."

In the meantime, Berlin fell to the Russians after days of savage combat with Nazi troops. On April 30, Adolf Hitler committed suicide in his concrete bunker beneath Berlin. And on May 7, Germany finally surrendered.

On V-E Day, "everybody just went wild, of course," says Helen Dixon Johnson, referring to May 8, 1945, Victory in Europe Day. Nurses joined the throngs of people celebrating in the streets of Paris and London; they were hugged, kissed, and treated like heroes.

The nurses were happy and relieved that the war in Europe was over; yet, they couldn't help thinking of all the young men they'd seen suffer and die.

Pauline Sommars remembers an ambulance arriving, full of newly released American POWs, including one man who was missing both legs. "He was hopping around, just on his stumps, and he was laughing and talking," she says. "He was so glad to be there. I could hardly hold back my tears."

And of course, the war with Japan raged on.

Because Helen Johnson was an operating-room nurse, she was scheduled to go to the Pacific, where her skills were badly needed. But she was ready to go home. "I wanted a good steak. I thought, if I ever get home, that's all I'm ever gonna have is steak."

Maureen Martin of the 128th Evacuation Hospital, on the other hand, was hoping to go to the Pacific after six months' leave in the States. She spent V-E Day at Camp Shanks, New Jersey. "We never did get to celebrate," she remembers, because they were not allowed to leave the base. "We sat on cots in this Army barracks and played Ouija board that night."

THE 95TH EVACUATION AND 51ST FIELD HOSPITALS: THE HORROR OF THE CAMPS

By 1945, Army nurses on the European front thought they had witnessed every horror of war. But for many, one more grisly scene awaited them: the concentration camps.

The Russians were the first to discover these camps where the Nazis sent Jews and anyone else they considered to be undesirable. Here the prisoners were either killed or put to work as slaves.

One such camp was Auschwitz in Poland. In this grim place, the Nazis murdered three million people in gas chambers. The dead included two million Jews, victims of Hitler's hatred.

In April, the Americans liberated Dachau, a camp near Munich, where more than 30,000 prisoners had been forced to work for the Nazis under brutal conditions and on very little food. Anyone too weak to work had died or been killed.

The nurses of the 95th Evacuation Hospital helped to care for the survivors, an experience Vera Rieck can hardly bring herself to describe. "To see those poor, starving people," she says, groping for words. "It was very, very, very sad."

Prisoners of Dachau Concentration Camp celebrate their liberation by U.S. troops on May 3, 1945. *(Hulton-Deutsch Collection/Corbis)*

Before entering the gates, the nurses were sprayed with DDT to ward off lice and disease. Inside they found the prisoners emaciated, like skeletons, and suffering from tuberculosis, typhus, lice, and dysentery. At mealtimes, the stronger patients came running at the smell of the food cart, devoured their meals, and begged for more.

Helen Dixon Johnson treated the survivors at Nordhausen, another labor camp in Germany. "I didn't know what I was getting into," she admits. "You could see hands sticking out of the ground." Stacks and stacks of corpses were heaped here and there awaiting burial; the living slept next to the dead, too weak to haul them away.

The patients "were just skin and bones," she says. "We had fields of them. They were so hungry and so starved, they hadn't seen a banana or an orange for I don't know how long. [Some] died because they were eating too fast. So we tried to feed them very slowly." Many were so weak and diseased that no amount of medical care could save them. They joined the approximately ten million people who died in the camps, including more than six million Jews.

ALICE IN THE PACIFIC: THE WAR'S NOT OVER YET

The war in Europe might have been over, but it wasn't in the Pacific. Alice Weinstein was now busy treating casualties in Zamboanga, in the southern Philippines, where MacArthur's forces were battling the Japanese. The 2nd Field Hospital was just a couple of miles from the front lines, and the nurses, housed in a library, had to be escorted by guards. "We were surrounded by

Japanese," Weinstein explains. "Japanese snipers would sit up in the trees; you couldn't see them."

At night, huge rats menaced the nurses. "You'd be asleep and all of a sudden these rats would be coming," Alice says. Each day, a soldier set out traps. "You'd just about go to sleep when you'd hear this CLACK! CLACK! CLACK! In the morning, you'd have all these dead rats."

Earlier that year, before moving to Zamboanga, the nurses had treated many patients suffering serious burns, victims of the increasingly frequent kamikaze attacks on U.S. ships. The closer the Americans drew to Japan, the more the suicide planes rained down on the fleet. In April, a kamikaze even struck the USS *Comfort,* a U.S. hospital ship, despite its being well illuminated and displaying the Geneva Cross. Six Army nurses were among the thirty people killed.

In March, the Marines captured the island of Iwo Jima in the bloodiest battle in Marine Corps history. Next, U.S. troops invaded Okinawa, a mere 360 miles from Japan, where it took them nearly three months to rout the determined enemy soldiers. More than twelve thousand Americans died in the fight; many more were wounded. (The wounded included a Marine named William Manchester, now a well-known writer. In his book *Goodbye, Darkness,* he describes the Army nurses as "freckled, rangy tomboys in baggy dungarees who laughed a lot, kidded us, and most important, knew when to say absolutely nothing.")

Now the only place left to invade was Japan itself, which the Americans dreaded. An invasion would cost a million American casualties, MacArthur estimated, not to mention countless Japanese civilian lives.

All through the spring, the Americans had pounded Japanese

The atomic bomb on August 9, 1945, flattened Nagasaki, Japan. *(National Archives/U.S. Air Force)*

cities with firebombs that set streets and homes ablaze, killing half a million people. Still, Japan refused to surrender.

On the morning of August 6, 1945, the Americans dropped an atomic bomb on the Japanese city of Hiroshima. The world had never seen such a bomb. It scorched the city, searing the earth and vaporizing anyone nearby. In an instant, four square miles of Hiroshima were left flat and blackened. A towering mushroom cloud rose over the city in a swirl of dust and wind. At least seventy-eight thousand persons were killed in the blast. Thousands more suffered terrible burns and radiation poisoning.

"If [the Japanese] do not now accept our terms," President Truman said, "they may expect a rain of ruin from the air, the like of which has never been seen on this earth."

On August 9, the United States dropped an atomic bomb on Nagasaki. That same day, the Russians invaded Manchuria, declaring war on Japan. On August 14, at the request of Emperor Hirohito, Japan surrendered.

"I really felt [the atomic bomb] was justified," says Alice Weinstein, speaking for many nurses. "You know, it sounds like you're cold and uncaring [to] say that, but when you're living in conditions where you're being bombed, and so many people are being killed, and you see the youths of America being maimed, then anything that's going to shorten the war seems justifiable to you, to us. And I think that's the way we felt, because all around us, we saw wards and wards of patients that were dying, that had permanent life injuries that they were going to have to learn to live with."

"We saw the youth of America just disappearing," adds another nurse.

Certainly many people disagree. Such a bomb can never be justified, they say. But the nurses saw the war as few people have, and have earned the right to their opinions.

Aboard the USS *Missouri*, General Douglas MacArthur signs documents making the Japanese surrender official as General Jonathan Wainwright looks on from behind. *(National Archives/U.S. Navy)*

August 15 was declared V-J Day. "I remember how excited everyone was," Weinstein says. "Each unit seemed to have fireworks and they were going off, and people were celebrating and dancing. People just couldn't get over it. When V-J Day finally happened, it was like an answer to a prayer."

On September 2, aboard the USS *Missouri* in Tokyo Bay, the Japanese signed formal surrender papers. "Skinny," General Jonathan Wainwright from Corregidor, was there at the surrender, having survived years of harsh imprisonment by the Japanese. After the signing, the sun broke out from behind the clouds. World War II was over at last.

ARMY NURSES AT HOME AND AFAR

Not all Army nurses served in the European or Pacific theaters. Many served in the 454 military hospitals in the United States. Their surroundings were familiar and comfortable, but their jobs were full  of challenges. Take nurse Betty Basye Hutchinson, for instance, who worked with GIs recovering from serious burns and amputations. Overseas, close to combat, these soldiers had been with people who understood their gruesome-looking injuries. But when Betty walked outside with a patient who had lost half his face to a firebomb, people stared with revulsion. It was up to nurses like Betty to help these men make the often difficult transition back to civilian life.[1]

A large number of nurses worked in Great Britain in the big station and general hospitals. Grace Hunn, a nurse with the 93rd General Hospital, remembers the Army instructing the nurses on proper behavior in England. "We were told, 'If you're invited to tea, be sure to go.'"

When General Eisenhower announced the success of the D day landings over the hospital loudspeakers, she says, "You've never heard such yelling and whooping. . . . I still get chills thinking about it." Soon after, "The wards started to fill up. From then on, we were very busy."

When my aunt, Army nurse June Bossler, was stationed in England, she tired quickly of Army fare like powdered eggs and brussels sprouts. One weekend, while visiting the local pub with some fellow nurses, she joined a group singing American songs. The locals loved her voice so much that right then and there they offered to pay her in fresh eggs, onions, bread, butter, and other fresh fare if she would only come in and sing on the weekends. June was shy, but she loved good food, so she agreed. After that, following her singing dates, she'd ride her bike back to camp, delivering her delicious loot to the eagerly awaiting nurses, who would quickly cook it up for their weekend treat.

June Bossler

(Edwinna Bernat)

Nurses also served in Iceland, Russia, Greenland, and in Liberia and the Belgian Congo in Africa. Approximately two hundred were stationed in Alaska, where they wore long underwear, coats, and lots of socks to stay warm. For fun, they learned to ski and snowshoe. Some went mushing (dogsledding) using the hospital's rescue dog teams. And in summer, the twenty-four-hour-a-day sunlight helped them to grow magnificent gardens. But those who were stationed in the Aleutians, that chain of islands that looks like Alaska's tail, saw almost nothing but fog.

The nurses stationed in the China-Burma-India theater would have welcomed a little of Alaska's cool air. Here, temperatures frequently rose above the one-hundred-degree mark, and nurses endured monsoons and dust storms.

For some nurses, service in Alaska meant sunlight twenty-four hours a day, while those who served in the Aleutians (that chain of islands that looks like Alaska's tail) saw almost nothing but fog. (ANC/U.S. Army)

In India, nurses enjoyed an occasional camel ride. They lived in little bamboo huts called bashas where they sometimes found one of the local cows inside, chewing her cud.

In Burma, where the Allies were fighting the Japanese, and Chinese troops were working with the Allies on a new supply route between India and China called the Ledo Road, the nurses sometimes found their Chinese patients rolling homemade noodles in the hospital. Elephant drivers who were working on the road occasionally showed up for outdoor movies—perched atop their elephants!

six

NOW THAT IT'S OVER

WHEN MARCELLA KORDA RETURNED TO THE UNITED STATES AFTER NEARLY three years overseas, "All I really wanted . . . was a glass of milk," she says. "La Guardia Airport was fogged in so we landed in Fort Dix, New Jersey. And do you think I could get a glass of milk that night? No!"

The staff of the 95th Evacuation Hospital, 1945. By this time, several nurses had left the unit, but three of the nurses from this book remained: Pauline Sommars (second row, far left); Marcella Korda (second row, fifth from left); and Vera Lee Rieck (second row, fourth from right). *(ANC/U.S. Army)*

When the war ended, nurses serving overseas headed in droves back to the United States, where they traded in their bedrolls for comfortable mattresses and their helmets for permanents. (ANC/U.S. Army)

Says Pauline Sommars, "The first thing I did when I got home from overseas was get a permanent. It felt so good." Of course, she notes, "It was kind of sad, leaving the unit." The staff had been through so much together.

While the nurses of the 95th Evacuation Hospital returned home in 1945, many other nurses remained in Germany or Japan with the Army of Occupation. The occupation forces helped to restore stability in the defeated nations, with the Medical Corps playing a particularly important role.

With so many cities bombed and so many people homeless, there was an enormous potential for epidemics of typhus and other diseases. Left unchecked, they could have killed thousands of people. The Army Medical Corps, along with relief organizations, helped to bring disease under control. By caring for German and Japanese civilians, the nurses also took some of the first steps toward healing the bitter feelings of the war.

When they returned home, many Army nurses continued nursing either in the military or the private health care industry. Alice Weinstein rejoined the Army Nurse Corps and rose to the rank of lieutenant colonel before retiring. Some, such as Helen Dixon Johnson, went back to school under the G.I. Bill of Rights, one of their benefits as veterans, using the education to further their careers. Johnson, for instance, obtained a master's degree from Columbia University, then worked for the Veterans Administration, retiring as assistant chief nurse for education and administration at a California veterans hospital.

"Don't call me a hero!" an Army nurse always says. "I was just doing my job."

Army nurses who served with the Army of Occupation in Europe helped to treat thousands of refugees left homeless by the war. Here a nurse works with children at a Polish displaced persons camp in Germany. *(ANC/U.S. Army)*

Alice Weinstein made her career in the Army Nurse Corps. In this 1960 photo, she was chief nurse of the Third Army. *(Alice Weinstein)*

Perhaps they are too modest. Every nurse who served in World War II, whether in a field hospital near the front lines or in a general hospital in the States, played an important role.

They proved, time and again, that women could work effectively under the most trying conditions. Mud, heat, bombs, long hours—it didn't matter. They had jobs to do, and they did them with courage and skill, regardless of the circumstances.

Most importantly, they helped to save lives. World War II was the first war in which more men died from combat than disease. Of those soldiers who received early medical care or swift evacuation for wounds or disease, less than 4 percent died. The nurses can take some of the credit for this impressive record.

More than fifty years have passed since World War II, and the Army Nurse Corps looks much different now. The quota system was abolished in 1944, and African American nurses have since joined the corps in great numbers. In 1979, Hazel W. Johnson became the first African American chief of the Army Nurse Corps. The corps now also includes male nurses, who have been eligible to serve since 1955.

Many nurses who served in World War II have died, but there are plenty left to tell their stories. Quite a few maintain close friendships with their fellow nurses and gather for reunions where they swap old stories.

Most of them remember their war experiences with pride and fondness. Although they saw more pain and death than anyone would ever want to see, it is the good things they choose to remember: the camaraderie among the staff, the jokes, the good cheer of the patients in the face of pain.

Unfortunately, many people have forgotten the nurses' contributions to the war. They don't know that they served under such trying, and even dangerous, conditions.

"When people learn I was in the war, they always ask, 'Were you a WAC?'" says one nurse.

But even the WACs are often overlooked in the history books. The same goes for almost all the women who have served or are serving in the military. For all their sacrifice, hard work, and valuable contributions, they have received little notice.

Brigadier General Wilma Vaught, retired from the Air Force, thought that women in the military deserved recognition and believed their stories needed to be recorded for future generations. Thus, she set to work on an ambitious project to honor them.

On October 18, 1997, thanks in large part to her efforts, the Women's Memorial opened at the gateway to Arlington National Cemetery in Washington, D.C. Here visitors can learn about Deborah

The Women's Memorial in Washington, D.C., honors United States servicewomen, past and present.
One of the memorial's architects, Michael Manfredi, is the son of a World War II Army nurse.
(Women's Memorial)

Sampson, who fought in the Revolutionary War disguised as a man. Or about Lieutenant Colonel Eileen Collins, who in 1995 became the first woman pilot of the space shuttle *Discovery*. And of course they can learn about the Army nurses and other women who served in World War II.

Using a computer database called the Register, visitors can retrieve information on thousands of military women, including most of the nurses in this book.

Vice President Albert Gore, speaking at the memorial's dedication, said, "At long last . . . we can unveil a memorial that says to every servicewoman, past and present, 'Thank you . . . for what you have done.'"

A long way from Anzio: Vera Rieck, Marcella Korda, and Lillie Homuth, from the 95th Evacuation Hospital, attended the dedication of the Women's Memorial in October 1997. "It's time the women in service were recognized," says Rieck, echoing the feelings of military women everywhere. (Vera J. Rieck)

★　　　★　　　★

Mildred Irene Clark, who treated the wounded during the attack on Pearl Harbor, became chief of the Army Nurse Corps in 1963. In 1964, she traveled to Detroit to give a speech. She was surprised to be placed in a luxurious suite at her hotel and greeted with an enormous bouquet of flowers. Naturally, she wanted to thank the hotel manager for such a kind welcome.

"You don't remember me, Colonel Clark," he said. "But I remember you. On the seventh of December, 1941, I was your patient."

More than twenty years had passed since then, yet he'd never forgotten the kind nurse who'd treated him. He could even describe what she'd worn that day. Says Clark, "It was nice to be remembered by a grateful patient."

Angels of Mercy, we remember you, too.

✪ BIBLIOGRAPHY ✪

Bellafaire, Judith A. *The Army Nurse Corps: A Commemoration of World War II Service.* Washington, D.C.: U.S. Army Center of Military History, 1993.

Bliven, Bruce, Jr. *The Story of D-Day: June 6, 1944.* New York: Random House, 1956.

Boylston, Helen Dore. *Clara Barton: Founder of the American Red Cross.* New York: Landmark Books, Random House, 1955.

Colman, Penny. *Rosie the Riveter: Women Working on the Home Front in World War II.* New York: Crown Publishers, 1995.

Feller, Carolyn M., and Constance J. Moore. *Highlights in the History of the Army Nurse Corps.* Washington, D.C.: U.S. Army Center of Military History, 1995.

Hakim, Joy. *War, Peace, and All That Jazz.* New York: Oxford University Press, 1995.

Holm, Jeanne M. *In Defense of a Nation: Servicewomen in World War II.* Washington, D.C.: Military Women's Press, 1998.

Krull, Kathleen. *V Is for Victory.* New York: Apple Soup Books/Alfred A. Knopf, 1995.

Leckie, Robert. *The Story of World War II.* New York: Random House, 1964.

Litoff, Judy Barrett, and David C. Smith. *We're in This War, Too: World War II Letters from American Women in Uniform.* New York: Oxford University Press, 1994.

Sullivan, George. *The Day Pearl Harbor Was Bombed: A Photo History of World War II.* New York: Scholastic, 1991.

Taylor, Theodore. *Air Raid—Pearl Harbor! The Story of December 7, 1941.* New York: Thomas Y. Crowell, 1971.

Terkel, Studs. *"The Good War": An Oral History of World War II.* New York: Pantheon Books, 1984.

Tomblin, Barbara Brooks. *G.I. Nightingales: The Army Nurse Corps in World War II.* Lexington: The University Press of Kentucky, 1996.

Vail, John J. *World War II: The War in Europe.* San Diego, Calif.: Lucent Books, 1991.

Wandrey, June. *Bedpan Commando.* Elmore, Ohio: Elmore Publishing, 1989.

Williams, Denny. *To the Angels.* San Francisco: Denson Press, 1985.

❂ ENDNOTES ❂

"WHAT IN THE WORLD IS GOING ON?"

1 Mildred Irene Clark's quotations were taken from an oral history maintained by, and used with the permission of, the Army Nurse Corps historian.

2 Unless otherwise noted, all quotations in the sections entitled "Ordeal in the Philippines" were drawn from oral histories maintained by, and used with the permission of, the Army Nurse Corps historian.

3 From *I Served on Bataan*, by Juanita Redmond, originally published by J. B. Lippincott, Philadelphia (1943); reprinted by Garland Publishing, Inc., N.Y., 1984.

4 The nickname Angels of Mercy was also bestowed upon women other than Army nurses, including, for instance, Red Cross workers.

REPORTING FOR DUTY

1 From *The Women's Army Corps: The U.S. Army in World War II*, by Mattie E. Treadwell, Office of the Chief of Military History, Washington, D.C., 1954.

"THE RAIN BEATING DOWN, THE GUNS FIRING"

1 Agnes Mangerich has written a book, *Albanian Escape*, published by the University of Kentucky Press, 1999.

"A CREDIT TO MY COUNTRY"

1 "Betty Basye Hutchinson," *The Good War*, by Studs Terkel, Pantheon Books, New York, 1984.

⊙ INDEX ⊙